BEST PRACTICE

BEST PRACTICE

Proven Strategies to Optimise Your Counselling Career for Immediate Success and Ultimate Succession

MERRILYN HUGHES

Published by Author Academy Elite
P.O. Box 43 Powell Ohio 43035
www.AuthorAcademyElite.com

Paperback ISBN13-978-1-946114-29-7
Hardcover ISBN13-978-1-946114-30-3

Library of Congress Control Number: 2016921131

For my family and friends,
Always my
Best People

CONTENTS

Section 3:
Embracing

Section 4:
Enduring

FOREWORD

In some circles around the world counsellors still struggle to be recognized as professionals.

We need more clear, competent, and confident mental health providers. My friend Merrilyn Hughes knows how to take us toward that goal. For years her practice was based on the three principles of synergy, sharing, and support. Throughout her career, Merrilyn has worked and supervised with these principles in mind. The success of her practice is a testament to these principles.

As part of her succession planning Merrilyn successfully mentored a young counsellor to take over and purchase her practice. This decision enabled Merrilyn to launch a new career as a writer, coach, mentor and speaker.

Her book—*Best Practice*—is a result of this new focus. It is a thought-provoking guide for counsellors to plan a practice that is both professional and successful from day one all the way through to ultimate succession.

Merrilyn explains how to become the best you possible before opening your practice, through self-exploration and the recognition of the values you take with you into the practice. This journey enables solid decision-making and clear goals.

Her nine-step comprehensive plan creates a counselling career hard-wired for achievement and growth.

Best Practice focuses on building a business that endures. This succession-planning component is a new challenge for counsellors who traditionally just wind down their practices. *Best Practice* is both a testament to a successful career and a giveback to the profession that Merrilyn has enjoyed so passionately.

Merrilyn expands upon these concepts in her *Best Practice* Program, providing further growth and development. This collaborative experience focuses upon the three principles of synergy, support, and sharing.

Now get ready to create a successful counselling career using the principles of Best Practice.

Kary Oberbrunner.
Author of Elixir Project, Day Job to Dream Job,
The Deeper Path and Your Secret Name

INTRODUCTION

As I walk into the waiting room, the tension grips me like a vice.

Nervousness and anxiety echo off the serene ocean scenes depicted in photographs on the walls. The ripples in the water under the jetty catch my eye, beautiful symmetry. I wonder if this client took the time to look and see. I smile, hoping to relieve some of the tension, and invite my client, the counselling profession, towards my office.

There is no eye contact.

I usher the counselling profession down the corridor and through the door and invite them to make themselves comfortable. They choose a large, black leather armchair, one of four in my office. I notice they use the chair closest to the door and sit precariously on the edge, hands clasped in their lap. I mirror this seating position with the hope of relaxing us both into the embrace of the comfy chairs. I take a couple of deep breaths, silently encouraging the client to follow suit, hoping the pause will create an interaction.

Still no eye contact.

"How can I help you today?" I coax gently.

The counselling profession wriggles, wrings their hands, uncomfortable, and then, after a long pause, offers, "I've felt this way for a long time."

I let silence surround us, enticing the client to elaborate without prompting. As the silence stretches, I prepare to cajole more from the client. I wait.

The client shuffles, sighs and the floodgates open.

The counselling profession begins describing a childhood with poorly defined boundaries, uncertainty and confusion, and shares that they still feel rudderless and unanchored, tossed about in the mental health ocean, unsure where they will dock. They look lost and forlorn.

They describe a relationship with their big brother, Psychology, to whom they have always felt inferior. Somehow, Psychology got all the recognition, the attention and the popularity, the favoured son, the golden child. There is an even more dysfunctional, distant relationship with their other sibling, Psychiatry. The client seems hesitant to discuss this connection.

The counselling profession slumps back in the chair, looking defeated. The voice has become almost a whine as the counselling profession explains to me they are unsure even who they are, where they fit in, and then describe just how confused and alone they feel.

They reveal that this feeling of isolation began the day they finished studying. They felt disconnected from the students and staff of the learning facility. They were alone in the big, wide world and felt unprepared for what was to come next. How were they supposed to help others when they felt so alone and isolated?

Still no eye contact.

I encourage the counselling profession to continue, keeping my own role minimal at this stage. They speak of many struggles, understanding how business works (and don't even mention tax accounting and marketing)—it is impossible to get clients! They continue with the fact that, with no income

– because there are no clients – they cannot afford to pay for ongoing professional development—whereas if they could afford to pay for it…they might be able to get clients. The words flood out in an unstoppable torrent.

"Ah, Catch 22?" I say.

This enables the client to bemoan the fact that all good, professional development requires plane flights as well as the cost of the course and with no clients…

We spend quite a bit of time and energy with the "poor me" scenario. It continues through the "Pay professional membership and get nothing from it" story to the "To stay registered there must be supervision and professional development" and back to "It's a struggle because there are no clients."

At this point, I sense an internal struggle; some parts are debating the issues. They know the answers; they know how to be professional; they can see the opportunities. I glimpse the well-dressed professional, confident and successful. Somehow, as a whole, the counselling profession just cannot get it together and the doubts overpower many.

I wait and watch this battle within, looking for some sign of self-awareness that may lead to solutions. There is a glimmer, but negativity wins and the client continues listing their woes.

We explore the times when the counselling profession becomes a "hobby" because, "We need a real job to pay the bills." This also means, "We work from the lounge room at home," or, "We volunteer for an agency to gain experience." Once again, these all end with, "We can't get clients."

I ask the counselling profession if they have ever had clients.

Now I get eye contact! I take the opportunity to reposition myself comfortably and the counselling profession follows suit.

Yes, they assure me, they have and they have done a great job when they have had clients, but those clients left and we are back to having no clients. This makes the counselling profession question their effectiveness.

I want to explore this further and ask, "How did you get these clients?"

The counselling profession explains that friends of friends were their first clients and then they advertised in the local paper. When that failed, they tried approaching their local doctor to set up referrals but they were not sure how to do this and were not very confident in their approach. In the end it amounted to nothing; it was a waste of time.

I ask point blank, "Is confidence an issue for you?"

The head drops and I lose the eye contact.

"Absolutely! It always has been. This was why we entered the counselling profession. We had things happen to us; we weren't confident; we want to help other people because we know how having no confidence feels."

"Who is in your support system when you feel like this?" I ask, looking for a positive spin.

"Well, we have a supervisor who we have to speak with and we do some free group supervisions because we can't afford individual supervision all the time." Oh, no! We are back to finances again! How do we go from wanting to help people to dollar signs so quickly all the time?

"What is the purpose of supervision?" I ask, trying to steer to a more functional aspect, less about finances.

The counselling profession perks up a bit here. They know the answer to this one! "To maintain professionalism," they say with a hint of pride. This feels incongruent with the rest of the session but it is positive. I think we should pursue this.

"So, what is professionalism?"

I suggest we look at this in the next session. I am confident the answer to this is not just that we seek it from our supervisors. I know I face many sessions with this client and I wonder exactly how invested they are in finding the answers they seek.

I set the homework task for the client to define professionalism and describe how this affects them.

The counselling profession leaves my room and I feel exhausted by the session.

I look down at the words I have written on my notepad during the session:

Anxious
Defeated
Pessimistic
Isolated
Low confidence
No self-esteem
Identity crisis
Rudderless
Professional?

As I begin writing up my session notes, I wonder how many times the counselling profession has dealt with these very issues with its own clients.

Cura te ipsum
Heal thyself

SECTION 1

MY EXPERIENCE IN A SELF-SABOTAGING PROFESSION

CHAPTER 1
BEGINNING

"My earliest memory is my mother coming home late at night, tired and short tempered. The dinner I had cooked earlier had dried out in the oven and Mum threw it in the bin. I was seven years old. There were just the two of us..."

I was not paying attention.

I was in a CBT tutorial, supposedly listening to this counselling scenario. The tutor was watching; a student was sharing a real life issue with the counsellor, also a student, and the rest of the group was observing ready to comment on the implementation of CBT techniques.

My mind was elsewhere. I was not paying attention.

Confusion will do that.

Earlier, during the tea break, I had been chatting, or probably more correctly listening into a group of six students, and the discussion turned to where we thought our studies would lead us.

The only guy in the group, let's call him Joe, a twenty-year-old who had experienced a lot in his years and was wanting to give back, thought he might like to "have a crack" at private practice, but felt he would probably end up working for an agency or maybe as a school counsellor. After all, a school counsellor had inspired him once.

Everyone sagely nodded his or her head. I wanted to say I thought he would make a great private practitioner; he had an empathy rarely seen in a man of his age. I guess schoolkids need empathy too. I kept quiet and listened.

Two women who I had seen at previous tutorials spoke rather sketchily about opening a weekend meditation retreat, maybe in the bush, by the beach or both. They giggled as they finished each other's sentences. They were concerned, however, that many such retreats already existed. Many of their friends went to Bali for these retreats now, which was much more cost effective. Maybe they would have to be more holistic; study reiki as well. Again all nodded in understanding and sympathy.

The next plan came from an ex-drug addict, Jan, possibly in her mid-thirties, who, frustrated by the lack of ongoing help when she had thrown the habit, wanted to help as a support worker for those travelling the same path. She just needed to find a vehicle for doing this work, maybe a church group or a not-for-profit. She was determined to volunteer as money was an issue for drug users.

In my head I was saying, *but if they have stopped using, surely they suddenly have disposable cash, don't they? They also have pride and dignity or, at the very least, need to build these. Sometimes value is important.* In my head, I questioned the word "help" but I kept my view to myself; maybe I was naïve or was I even being judgemental?

Then there was Grace. Grace hoped to set up a private practice but doubted that she would have the business acumen to succeed. Hadn't we all seen the headline quoting the Australian Bureau of Statistics who said 44 small businesses close in Australia every day? Counselling was one thing; business was another.

I suggested maybe doing a small business course and was surprised with the reply that it would make more sense to buy a small retail business to run because a counselling future was not guaranteed. Had we not just all nodded agreement that there were no guarantees in a small business? My internal dialogue was in overdrive!

The attention turned to me. What was I going to do with my study? I was going to open a practice of course. Everyone looked at me. I felt judged as strange, vain or maybe insane! The holistic ladies looked at each other and smiled. The consensus seemed that I was brave, but I interpreted that as crazy. No one was nodding!

As I sat in the tutorial, I replayed the sequence of future expectations over in my head. Why were they settling? They had given up even before they had even started, even tried. Two of my favourite Michael Jordan quotes came to mind. I wrote them down.

"I can accept failure, but I cannot accept not trying."

"You have to expect things of yourself before you can do them."

These students were not really trying; they had low expectations. I felt they were on the road to failure before they even became qualified. I did not want to share their journey.

The role-play had finished, everyone was heading out for lunch. I walked in the opposite direction. I looked at my critique sheet. All I had were the two Michael Jordan quotes. I would have to fly by the seat of my pants in the discussion later. *Maybe I should check in with some of the others over lunch.* I decided against this. I was still confused and felt deflated. I needed time for reflection and went for a walk by the river.

Was I fooling myself?

I walked and picked at the sandwich I had made for lunch. I ate without tasting. I knew what I wanted. Why did it now feel doubtful and even unrealistic? I reminded myself that this was my decision, and, while others were entitled to opinions, I did not have to buy into them. This was my dream!

With my mother's voice ringing in my ears, "A job worth doing is worth doing well," I decided there and then, that day on my walk by the river, I was opening a practice as soon as I could and it would be the best practice it possibly could be. I would be the best counsellor I possibly could be.

I did not need nodding.

❧

The decision I made that day became my motivation. The Michael Jordan quotes became my mantras. I had always been a prolific reader, but now I could not get enough. I did all the prescribed reading, read many of the books cited in our readings. I subscribed to journals and scoped the Internet for topics on which I wanted more information and knowledge.

I made a plan. I was going to be experienced and ready to open a practice. I networked with people in the field; volunteered as a support worker; worked on a help line; soaked up all the training I could get and attended all the professional development I could. My study became only a small part of my learning.

One day, I was attending a workshop on culture and diversity run by a government department. As often happens in some workshops, the facilitator invited us to share why they were doing the training. There were about twenty people attending the workshop from many different workplaces. Most were doing the workshop because it was a requirement for their jobs. Only two of us did not fit this mould—me, who wanted to learn as much as possible, and a young Islamic woman.

I was intrigued, as were most of the others, as to why a mother of two young children, refugee and such a young woman, was doing a course such as this. Her motivation was that she was doing anything she could to understand the way of thinking in her new country. She also had a plan!

This woman and I became friends on that day and continue to be today, although she now has moved interstate. Our emails are always interesting and I learn from her every time. She is now studying philosophy and continues her quest for knowledge and understanding.

I really like her plan!

I have reflected often on the difference between this woman's plan and the plans of the students that day in the CBT tutorial. Success is a road we pave for ourselves.

⁍

Our Graduation day arrived.

I took the day off from my practice, put on what I thought was a graduation appropriate outfit, and turned up excited to catch up with some of the students I had studied with over time. I had stayed in touch with several of these fellow graduates via email and was hoping that, unlike them, some of the other graduates were working in the field. I saw this as an opportunity to network.

All armed with our certificates, duly hand shaken, photographed and congratulated by family and friends, graduates mingled. We reminisced about days with heads in books, laughed at our naïve attempts at some of the practical exercises we had completed and began talking of the "So, what are you doing now?" conversations.

Somehow, however, I was prepared to be disappointed.

Joe was waiting to hear back about a school chaplain job at a school in the southwest. He decided against "having a crack" at setting up a practice as he had heard it was difficult to get started. He was looking forward to working with kids, though the girls frightened him a bit.

The "holistic" girls were not at graduation but someone had heard they had enrolled to study reiki and natural medicine. Similarly, Jan, who wanted to peer support ex drug users, was not present but was working as a volunteer with a not-for-profit doing administration as a foot in the door to becoming a peer supporter.

Grace had set up a private practice in a shared office with another counsellor but had to leave due to a lack of clients. She was seeing a couple of clients in her home office, although she was finding this lonely. She was considering going to university to study something else maybe.

I shared the opening of my practice and described the work I had been doing both in my office and out in the field. The consensus was that I was lucky it had all worked out for me. There was much head nodding and I just went along with the flow of conversation.

I did not tell them about the hours of research, the writing of programs, the many phone calls I made, and emails I had sent, both before and since finishing my study, and this was really just the tip of the iceberg! Why not just put it down to luck!

I spoke with many other graduates that day, looking for someone who was happy with where their study had taken them. I was both disappointed and frustrated with the mentality of many of the graduates. An absolute minority of the graduates were positive about their futures.

I also spoke with some of the academics, and was surprised at their surprise on hearing of the progress in my practice. How can they teach without belief?

❧

I hunted for about a month to find some suitable premises for my practice. I had set criteria in my search. I was determined not to have a home office; this to me did not feel professional. I was also protective of my family home and my sanctuary. Nor did I want a practice annexed with a medical practice. Much of counselling work is relationship orientated and many people do not want that in the same breath as mental health issues. I was looking for independence, somewhere clients would feel anonymous but also somewhere with a profile.

I wanted somewhere easily accessible, yet discreet, with a room big enough for workshops and seminars. I wanted more than one office so I could have someone work in the business with me when the client list demanded. I also knew that I was a person who needed space.

This was a challenge but eventually I found an office and warehouse facility in an industrial estate. It was centrally located, on a bus route. The warehouse converted into a workshop and conference room easily and I actually had three offices and a waiting room. It felt very professional.

I was very happy with my choice of location but had a few doubters who thought an industrial estate was not the right environment for a practice. I was not completely convinced myself, but we would see.

The lease on my practice began the day I finished my course. I was impatient and did not even wait for graduation so I had my 'piece of paper for the wall'. My piece of paper was the registration of my business.

My practice, especially in concept, had started months before that when I sought help from a small business development group. It was a free group run by the government and I used their template to complete a business plan. I spent many, many hours on this business plan that I adapted to suit a counselling practice; it was the blueprint for my business and I needed to get it right. I needed to succeed.

I had worked on a multitude of concepts, which challenged me: business ethos, designing logos, purpose, mission statements, objectives, finance, competition, marketing strategies, client profiles, team building with other professionals like accountants, lawyers, insurance brokers; the list seemed endless.

There were times when I felt overwhelmed by all the decision-making and these days would send me walking by the river to refocus, Michael Jordan whispering in my ear. "Expect things of yourself."

CHAPTER 2
PRACTISING

I clearly remember the first working day in my office. I walked in, unlocked the door to my office and sat in the new leather office chair at my desk. I got up, filled the water jug and put out the glasses. I checked the tissues, which I already knew were a new box, and moved both the black leather chairs so they faced each other a little more. My first client was only an hour away. Tears rolled down my cheeks. How was I going to do this? I could not stop crying, though I was not sure whether it was for joy, for fear, out of relief or simply because I was so very exhausted!

I washed my face and waited tentatively for my client to arrive at ten.

At five past ten, every bit of doubt I had seen in others was in my heart. My client had not turned up! I was not going to allow this to defeat me and I checked my calendar for the client's number. I called her. I heard the ring tone, she was walking through the door, madly apologising for being late.

I felt sure she could physically feel my relief! Doubt disappeared.

That first hour of counselling went so fast it was frightening. There was so much to think about afterwards I was not sure where to start. I wrote up my session notes and dot pointed out a treatment plan, pleased with myself as I filed the client file.

I would definitely have to work on the note making. I looked up to see my one o'clock appointment arrive as I locked the filing drawer. Oh well, I would just have a late lunch.

I was on my way. My plan was in full flight.

I was extremely happy in my practice; I had clients trickling in during my first week at the office. This built to a steady flow within a month and I soon settled into the rhythm of working sessions with my clients, developing programs and running workshops.

These first few clients came mostly from talks I had given at the local high school about exam anxiety and study techniques. The students had just finished their mid-year exams and many of them had listened to the free 20-minute chat I had given. Some of these students were working way below their capability due to anxiety or poor study routines. Because they had my contact details on the handout I distributed at the talk, they knew where to turn to for help.

I am not going to pretend it was easy. Yes, the things people had said were true—clients did not come beating a path and knocking at the door all by themselves. However, they did exist. All around me were people in need of some solid counselling.

I celebrated when, on day 21 of my practice, I received my first referral from an existing client. This was one of my early business goals and I certainly did not expect it to happen so quickly. All goals suddenly seemed more achievable. I was over the moon!

❧

Once the doors were open, I had yet to address two things—firstly supervision and, secondly, professional development, which are both a requirement of being registered.

I looked at the list of supervisors recommended by the Counselling Association and decided to try three of them out. Two were local, the third was interstate, and I was to contact via phone.

The first local supervisor was difficult to get an appointment with but I persevered and when I attended my first session I was glad I had. There was an instant rapport and I felt I had made a great decision. This was short-lived, however, as the supervisor explained that she was retiring and really thought I would be better off with a different supervisor.

The second supervisor I tried was the interstate phone supervisor. I felt detached, felt this supervisor was not supportive and suspected that he was multi-tasking as there was a lot of clatter from his end. This was definitely not for me.

The third attempt was with a local counsellor. We worked well in our first session so I decided to stay with her for supervision. I worked with her for a couple of years but never really felt challenged.

None of the supervisors I saw in those early years challenged me. I felt like I knew more than they could teach me, though I always went into each session hopeful. I celebrated the rare occasion I came away with new insight, especially if it led to further research.

At no point did any of my supervisors enter into a discussion regarding the business side of my practice. I found this both disappointing and frustrating. I became more determined to succeed as a business and sought answers for myself.

I began going to Counselling Association meetings, as one way to achieve the professional development I needed to remain registered. I only attended these sporadically as they were on at one of the busiest times for me in my practice, Saturday mornings. Unfortunately, it meant missing not only the professional development but also an opportunity to network with other counsellors.

Professional development had never been a challenge for me. I was constantly studying and read excessively when challenges presented themselves to me. This was boundless in the early days and has never waned, not even in retirement.

Much of my logged professional development came from interstate conferences. For me these were an opportunity to learn, a chance to network and an opportunity for downtime. A two-day conference often became a three or four-day break. Over time, besides the invaluable learning, I was fortunate to meet some very interesting people at these conferences.

One particular annual conference saw me seated next to a social worker from Tasmania. We hit it off. As we were both staying at the hotel that the hosted conference, we decided to catch up for dinner. We had a wonderful, challenging discussion about inner child work. This was the beginning of a wonderful friendship and a professional alliance that lasted for years. We often reflect on how much we both learned from our time together at the conferences and from each other.

∾

My practice progressed, meeting some of the goals set in my plan and struggling with others. These became my challenges. There was always work I needed to do. I recognised that running a practice involved more than seeing the clients who walked through the door.

I subleased one room in my office to my supervisor who was having difficulty finding a suitable office. It was good to have company and saved me driving time when I needed supervision. This worked well until the need to make more money made her decide to go back to her bookkeeping roots. I missed her company and once again was in search of a supervisor.

My focus became marketing. There are ethical restrictions on advertising in the counselling profession but marketing can take many forms. Being situated in an industrial estate leant itself to setting up some Employee Assistance Programs (EAPs) with some of the local businesses. This is where employers provide free counselling for their employees in the interest of a healthy, productive workplace.

I did a letterbox drop, followed up with phone calls and, if businesses were interested, I would personally visit to present my program. It certainly made for some interesting meetings!

This created a regular supply of clients for my practice. The work was as diverse as the businesses were varied. Some of the work was run-of-the-mill counselling work but some was not. The interesting work included working with victims of workplace accidents, both at the scene and in follow up. EAPs also opened the door to a series of 20-minute talks to employees on topics like work/life balance, communication and time management.

I really enjoyed this work as it took me out of the office and into different workplaces, allowing me to meet a variety of people and once again forcing me to expand myself through research.

I was astonished when, at an Association group supervision, one counsellor announced that only psychologists should carry out EAP work. The big EAP providers only used psychologists. I challenged this and asked who decided rules such as these—psychologists? I wonder why we put these limitations on our profession. Do we not feel good enough? Who is making us feel this way?

One of the most interesting clients came years after the letterbox drop. The client had kept the flyer pinned to the company noticeboard, just in case. Unfortunately, there was an industrial accident on site and the client had reached for the flyer immediately. I worked with the shocked workers on the site that day and in the following weeks worked with the victim's family at his bedside, worked with the victim through his physical recovery and worked with management through the stress of the workplace investigation. All because I letter dropped a flyer.

I also engaged many clients through the workshops I wrote and ran. I ran quite a variety of workshops in the early days while I found my feet and tested the market interest. Some were more successful than others were, all were on my learning curve and some bring a smile to my face even today.

One such workshop was a 'Reignite your Romance' workshop for couples. This was a light-hearted look at relationships with the goal of finding the spark again. One night, while working through answers couples had written in their books, we came to the question 'What is romance?' The entire workshop ended up in hysterical laughter when we realised all eight men had written a comment about sex and all eight women had written comments about emotions. Much hilarity ensued and yet I think we all learned something that night!

Another avenue for acquiring clients came quite out of the woodwork. I received a phone call one day from a local veterinarian clinic. They requested my presence to assist with a client of theirs who had just lost her dog, and best friend. I drove the short distance to the clinic and the receptionist escorted me into a room where a woman sat with a dog on her lap. She was very distraught. I mostly just sat with her.

The clinic asked if they might have a few business cards to pass out to their clients as needed and I gladly obliged. Next thing I knew I was on the Veterinarian Board webpage as a preferred provider of counselling services for animal lovers suffering from grief!

This led to work from several vet clinics and this evolved even further when one of the clinics that referred to me lost one of their workers to suicide. The practice manager asked me to talk to the staff of this clinic about compassion fatigue and self-care.

I knew little about this topic and spent the week prior to my talk researching and writing a program to offer to this workforce. I was both astounded and horrified at the feedback from this program. Many of the staff members were at risk and the practice manager shared my concern. I set up an EAP and this became one of the busiest times for my practice. This enabled the staff to work through their grief for their lost workmate, learn self-care strategies and set up a better communication and support system within the workplace.

Soon other clinics and animal welfare groups requested my program, I set up EAPs and more work flowed. The veterinary industry, it seemed, was small and communication was big. It was time to get someone in to help.

This was the decision that caused me much concern. Whom could I trust to work in my practice? I had always trusted my decisions but for some reason this caused me great unease. Maybe it was just the fact that I had worked so hard and now was taking a risk or maybe it was just the control freak in me!

I had had counsellors fill in stopgaps before but none of these were available, so I would have to start from scratch. For the first time since I opened the practice I found myself procrastinating, resisting this next step. Progress, it seemed, was crippling me.

As so often happens in times of dilemma, the solution became apparent when I stopped looking. I met a very experienced and like-minded counsellor at an Association meeting, and, after meeting for a coffee chat, we began a trial. We fitted well together and began working in tandem. My practice was growing, another goal achieved.

This led me to discover that, while clients were in and out of the office all day, the constancy of another counsellor in the workplace was energising. I had company, someone to bounce ideas off, and I was free to write more programs and workshops.

It was during this time I also did my training as a supervisor. Initially, I did this training to discover exactly what a supervisor's role was supposed to look like. I still felt let down by the whole supervision concept. I discovered that supervision was an area I enjoyed and felt I could provide other counsellors with the assistance and challenges they needed to grow as counsellors.

I felt that the practice had a second life and soon we were both busy most of the time. We worked well together and I was encouraged to speak of another part of my business plan, succession. This counsellor had all the traits I was looking for to become a partner now, and then sell the practice to when I was ready to retire. We discussed the idea over lunch one day and it went well. She just had to discuss it with her husband and we would go from there.

The following week we discussed the idea again. She was very keen but I sensed some hesitation. I was upfront and mentioned my concern to her and she said she would have to discuss it with her husband again. I was confused but not concerned.

She came into my office first thing the following Monday with the news that she and her husband were moving back to their hometown in New Zealand and she was going to have to leave the practice. I was sad to lose a great colleague and missed her dreadfully when she left. While I refused to let this upset me, I felt deflated at the thought that my first attempt at growing my practice had ended this way.

～✦～

I slipped back into solo mode and took some time to regroup. The workload was horrendous. This was surely only going to be a short-term solution. I stopped all research (for the first time I could remember since I began studying!), put the marketing on the backburners and just focused on clients and workshops. This was more than enough and I reminded myself daily about burnout and compassion fatigue. I felt I was walking a very fine line!

One weekend, during this time, I was delivering a compassion fatigue workshop to a group of animal welfare volunteers who had recently been involved in rescuing and often euthanizing animals from a local bushfire. Many of the volunteers showed effects of trauma and overwork. Most of them would not have it any other way. These were very dedicated animal lovers.

I was working through a questionnaire with them all, looking at symptoms of both burnout and secondary trauma. As I read them out, I marked my own copy. Alarm bells rang! I put it aside while I finished the workshop and promised myself I would look closely at it that evening.

As happens, life got in the way and it was Monday morning in the office before I rediscovered the sheet. I sat there and decided to analyse the questionnaire as though it belonged to a client. I wrote down my recommendations for this client, reshuffled my clients for the week and took a week off to sit at our holiday house on the beach.

I rested up and did a lot of naval gazing for two days then wrote a self-care program for when I went back to work. I also recognised the fact that I could no longer do this alone. I needed to find a counsellor to help in the business.

I also made a huge decision during this time.

I was going to retire from counselling in June 2016! This gave me a year! This was an enormous decision for me as it felt like I was losing a child. My practice had been my baby, my focus, and I really was heart tied to it. My plan had not foreseen this!

CHAPTER 3
ENDING

My original business plan had a succession plan in it and I was so pleased I had worked through this at a time when emotion had not tied me to the practice. I knew I had planned based on logic and not emotion.

I set about finding someone who met the requirements I had set out in the succession plan. By this time, I had several contacts, many counsellors I supervised and felt sure I would find the person I was seeking. I decided that I would begin my search at the monthly Association meeting, where I was now holding group supervisions. I prepared an application form to find out who was available and wanted to work in my practice. I never had to use this form because, the day before the meeting, I had a private supervision session and, as so often happens, opportunity solved my dilemma.

So began a period of mentoring, monitoring and managing the new recruit. My plan had always been to pick a good counsellor, but someone who needed support to get into and run a successful private practice. I knew how hard this was to do flying solo. Many counsellors had told me often enough how difficult it was to start a practice. This recruit would always be ahead of the game because of the sharing of knowledge, the existence of client lists and the infrastructure of a solid business already established.

Some days I felt I had made a mistake; my practice was still my baby. I agonised over whether I had chosen the right person to care for my practice. I was confident in their counselling skills but the very criteria I had used for finding someone was causing me to doubt my decision.

One of the criteria I used was that the recruit I chose needed to lack confidence, needed mentoring to succeed. I questioned this criteria many times during the first months. Was I shooting myself in the foot? What was I thinking?

I also think at this time I was suffering a little from 'empty nest' syndrome as my children were leaving home at the same time. All my babies were moving on, flexing their wings.

I went back to my plan on many an occasion to remind myself that I set this criteria for a reason. The day at the CBT tutorial had shown me the lack of confidence in this profession. My succession plan included helping at least one counsellor overcome this hurdle. Yes, I felt I had made a good decision and stopped doubting to focus on moving forward with my plan.

Teaching a recruit the day-to-day running of the practice was something I found easily achievable over time. We entered into discussions about taking over the practice and anxiety was thick in the air. I knew I was really challenging this recruit and many times, I felt her desire to walk away, saw it in her unshed tears.

I introduced her to some of my support people, my accountant in particular. My accountant did not understand the reasoning behind putting someone so lacking in confidence in charge of my baby. My hope is that, over time, my confidence in her will rub off and prove to the accountant that I made a good decision.

My accountant's other concern was how to value the practice for sale. She searched for precedence and came up empty-handed. Evidently, counsellors do not sell their practices; they just wind them up. My accountant agreed I had a very sellable asset and we began the process of valuation. Once again, my accountant also did not understand that market price was not what I was aiming for; it was irrelevant to my plan.

I wanted to sell my practice for its value to its new owner. Market value would just feed the anxiety. By now, the recruit was invested, had agreed to buy and I was convinced I had made the right choice. The price seemed quite irrelevant to me. It felt like profiting from a child and a little unethical.

This really went against the strong business acumen I had tried to have in the practice. I knew I was acting against the professional advice of my accountant but it felt so right. I discussed this with the accountant and we decided on a figure below market value but enough for the new owner to value the practice for what it was.

As I write this, the doubt seeps back in for a nanosecond. I have risked a lot, and yet nothing, because in giving the practice real value, I have happily moved on to the next part of my life.

I encountered many an amazed counsellor, supervisee and peer when I shared the news of my retirement from counselling. Greater amazement, however, came at the notion of selling my practice.

The abnormality of selling the practice became even clearer to me, however, when I met with the liaison officer from the Counselling Association. I mentioned that I was selling the practice and he was surprised. He had never heard of someone selling their practice; you just close them down. I cannot understand how counsellors value their practices, or rather do not value them. This conversation was the convincer that led me to writing this book.

When a representative of your professional body doesn't recognise the value of a practice, when counsellors themselves don't value a practice, and sometimes their life's work, enough to put it to the market, when as a profession we don't pass on what we have learned and created to the next generation of counsellors, how do we expect the outside world to see us as professionals? Are we acting as professionals?

I feel I did.

Professio superbio
Professional pride

SECTION 2
EVOLVING

CHAPTER 4
SETTING UP

I am not aware of any people, in any other businesses, who, in the process of setting up, decide that there is a limited lifespan for the proposed business right from the outset. Neither have I heard of a businessperson who does not expect the business to outlive them when they are in the process of setting it up. Mechanics set up shop with every intention of selling the shop or leaving it to a family member to carry on the business. Even the owner of the local corner shop expects to sell the business at some stage.

I think this is especially true, however, when it comes to professional businesses.

Can you imagine a lawyer setting up business just for the term of his working life, or a doctor, a physiotherapist, an accountant, an engineer? A lawyer setting up a new law firm would certainly envision a long life for the firm, whether through generational succession or through the introduction of partners. And this is regardless of whether the business is in a large city or the smallest country town.

Like counsellors, these professionals have studied hard and long to achieve their positions. There is value in their qualifications. There is also value in their professional and business achievement. There is value in their loyal clients, the long-term contracts and the respected name of their firm.

It seems self-defeating to limit the lifespan of a professional business, not to mention a waste of resources, particularly knowledge. I have seen a lot of evidence that suggests many counsellors set up their practice not even focusing on the fact that it is a business, let alone that it is a saleable, enduring asset.

Nor do I know of any other successful business that sets up without doing the figures to determine profitability. Many counselling practices start this way with little forethought. Somehow, practices are set up just believing things will work out without much consideration at all as to the market, the competition, the optimum setup or the insight into how advertising might work.

If we think of our practices as businesses then we are more inclined to act as business people. If, however, we think of our practice as a hobby, we are enthusiasts. Is this not the Law of Attraction we espouse to many of our clients? Think, as you desire to be. Do, as you desire to be. Let us look at what it takes to set up a business and how the counselling profession can join other professions in creating strong, recognised businesses.

❦

Setting up any business begins with research, lots of research, research on many different things—from demographics, market, existing services, demand and location, down to company ethos, name and logos. I found that, for this research, a formatted document works best, usually a business plan.

Putting up a shingle does not guarantee success; having a diploma, degree or masters does not guarantee success; doing hours and hours of reading does not guarantee success. Moreover, having life experiences of your own certainly does not guarantee success.

Success is multi-faceted. It is true that without qualifications, success is unachievable; without somewhere to practice, success is unachievable; without specific knowledge, success is unachievable. It is a combination and a culmination of these many facets that guarantees success.

This is not true only of counselling practices. A motor mechanic is limited without qualifications, knowledge and a workshop, even if he has pulled an engine to pieces, just as a hairdresser is or a lawyer.

So, where to start? I would like to break it down into two main parts, bringing the best you and having the best plan, which consists of the nine Ps of practice planning—preliminaries, purpose, products, price, place, promotion, people, processes and profitability.

CHAPTER 5
THE BEST YOU

First, choose the best you for the job. Sounds simple, doesn't it? What is the best you for your business and practice? After years of study, do you know what you personally need from your practice, what your practice needs from you personally?

The first step is very much one of self-discovery. Let us look at how you can become a great business and professional you by focusing on being a great you.

The essence of any person is a combination of different values. We all have our own set of values and within our set; we have values that differ for each separate area of our life. For example, our values when we socialise with family members is different to those we have when we are with friends and different again when we are in the professional arena. Yes, the core value is the same, but how we apply it differs.

Let's look at the value of appreciation. In the family setting appreciation might mean affectionately embracing a family member; in a friendship situation we may buy a gift to show appreciation; in a professional situation, although we still want to show appreciation, neither of these methods may be suitable, maybe it is a smile and a handshake, or a monetary reward.

To understand how these values might differ, we first have to recognise what our core values are, and how our professional values differ from our personal ones. Some people know their core values and may feel they do not need to look into this and that is OK.

Establishing or reviewing your values is challenging but also inspiring and can be very fulfilling. It is important to recognise that values are not static; they are ever changing; your values of ten years ago are not your values today.

For me one of my core values today is accountability. This means being true to me, showing others the real me. In my friendships it means being honest and integral. In business it means being able to back my word with facts, being open and genuine. If indeed this was a core value for me in my twenties, it certainly meant something quite different.

If you would like to explore your values, I have shared here a method I found works well for me. To establish or revise your core values I like to use the HEART acronym.

H is for history.

We are not born with values. We originally learn these from those who raise us, by watching and learning what is acceptable. As we grow others influence our values, teachers, peers, siblings, media- wherever you spent your time, there was influence on your value set. Whether you kept these or rejected them and replaced them with something else, you have developed a set of core values, ready to evolve with you through your life.

Think about what values you learnt about money, status, success, achievement, education, work ethic, your appearance, independence, sports and hobbies, love and relationships, sexuality, culture, family and religion. Write down what you learned growing up.

Which of these values did you challenge? Which were negotiable? Are any of them still in their original state? How have they developed?

The value of family is a very strong value for me, as it was for my parents, as I hope it is for my children. I remember distinctly the sadness of the first Christmas I was not at home. My husband and I had moved to live in Papua New Guinea and did not have leave in December. I was devastated, as was my mother, who had managed to have all seven of her children with her every Christmas until that year. The change was inevitable, we both accepted this, but it challenged our value of family. Now, as my children have all left home, I have faced my first Christmas not having them all around. That value of family, I now realise is still as strong as ever; it just looks different. I now share my mother's perspective.

E stands for explore.

Take this opportunity to search for the people and things in your life that have inspired you, the personality traits you admire in others, behaviours that you find acceptable and those you don't. Explore what upsets you, what makes you smile, what makes you feel angry, what you can and cannot tolerate. Look at the boundaries you set for yourself, for your relationships and for your interactions with others. Think about how others see you, talk to them if necessary. Why do you get up every morning? What can't you live without in your life? What rules have you made that no longer work for you? What would your perfect day look like?

An exercise I found helpful in this exploration was to set the table for twelve people. In the first setting, with whom would you most like to share a meal? People you admire, people who inspire you and people whom you have something in common. Then, have a look at the people you would like to least share a meal with. Look at why these two groups, they tell you a lot about yourself.

Another simple exercise is to pack a suitcase. You may only take 12 things forward with you into a new world. What would you pack? There is a good reason you choose the things you choose. Look at what value these things reflect.

Explore all these things and as many more as you can think of. This is an ongoing process. I recently found myself smiling to myself watching two teenage boys both trying to impress the same girl. I caught myself and questioned why I smiled at this. After thinking about it, I came up with two values that I hold close. The first is that love for others makes us complete, and the second is that competition is healthy. The storyteller in me also wonders how they both ended up, was the girl interested, and in which one.

Asses all the information you have put together so far. Can you see some clear patterns? It is time to identify your own core values. Use the information you have gathered and try to list twenty values that resonate for you.

Here are some examples of core values from which you may wish to choose:

Dependable, Reliable, Loyal, Committed, Open-minded, Consistent, Honest, Efficient, Innovative, Creative, Humorous, Fun-loving, Adventurous, Motivated, Positive, Optimistic, Inspiring, Passionate, Respectful, Athletic, Fit, Courageous, Educated, Respected, Loving, Nurturing, Authentic, Helpful, Balanced, Humble, Original, Courteous, Affectionate, Congruent, Passionate, Trustworthy, Sensual, Kind, Truthful, Sincere, Thoughtful, Religious, Family, Dignity, Brave, Cooperative, Generous, Open.

This is by no means a complete list and some of your values deserve your own description. Discover your own list. Many values cannot be described in one word either.

Reflect on the information you have gathered up to this point, look at the values you have identified. If necessary, clarify them, personalise them, and make them your own. These values are your guide to life, your moral compass. They reflect who you are and what you stand for. They reveal what is important to you, what really matters.

T is for testament. This is where you commit to these values. Write a statement that includes:

How you intend to honour your values
How you will realign to these values when they are challenged
How and when you will revisit these values
Your promise to you to live by these values.

HEART is a long process, but your values are the basis of how you live. Therefore, they become the basis for how you will practice in business. Take your time to develop your list of values and revisit it often.

Once you are confident with your core values, it is important to realise how these will affect your professionalism and your practice. Look at your top twenty values. Evaluate how the application of these values might differ in the work environment. For example if perseverance is one of your values, then how will this translate in the counselling room? Is perseverance always in the best interest of your client?

How can these values best serve you in your practice? Values such as compassion and caring are wonderful assets in both your personal life and your professional practices, but beware of the pitfalls. It has been well documented that compassion fatigue is a very real concern for therapists today.

Other factors influence our values in the professional environment. An association's code of ethics is a set of values for a profession. We need to ensure that our values and the governing body's values are congruent. If they are not, then something needs to change, either your working value or maybe find an association who shares your values. I know this sounds unlikely to happen, but some cultural beliefs can make the interpretation of some association code of ethics feel uncomfortable.

Knowing your values is a great start to knowing yourself. It is the foundation. The next step is to discover what these values have enabled you to do so far in life. You can accomplished simply by completing a Strengths/Weaknesses/Opportunities/Threats (SWOT) analysis.

We best achieve this by recognising a strength and expanding it through the three other categories as in Diagram 1. Follow this procedure for all strengths, weaknesses, opportunities and threats. Be as honest and open as possible as this will enable you to come away with a clear picture of yourself. If you have trouble establishing strengths, weaknesses, opportunities or threats, ask people close to you to give their opinion to help you. These should be long and distinguished lists.

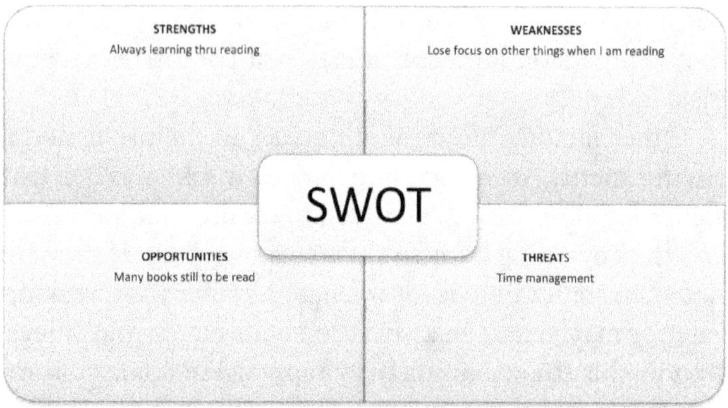

Diagram 1. SWOT Analysis.

This SWOT exercise should allow you to discover personal strategies for being an effective practitioner. If you discover attributes, you would like to change then seek the help to facilitate the change. For example, the threat in Diagram 1 may benefit from a time management strategy such as a weekly planner.

To be the best counsellor, it is vital that we comprehensively deal with any personal issues as much as possible. Many counsellors decide to become counsellors because of their own experiences. While some peer support can be beneficial for a client, we should be careful not to muddy the waters with our own issues. When we practice with outstanding issues, they can get in the way and prevent full focus on the client. Ongoing therapy, as well as supervision is a great idea for those who have a history of issues.

Beginning a new practice, like starting anything new, can cause some anxiety. The more prepared you are personally, and professionally the more confident you will be to take the next step. If anxiety or self-doubt become a problem, find solutions so you can effectively move forward. Ignore these first signs at your own peril. Anxiety grows, and if you do not nip it in the bud, in can become a large weed in your garden.

I have seen, too often, counsellors with diminishing confidence struggle to set up practices. It is counter-productive and once on the slippery slope, it is difficult to return. These areas of our personal life need exploring to become good practitioners. There is much to say for getting your ducks in a row before you begin and as author Stephen Covey says, "Begin with the end in mind." If you want a successful business present as a successful person from the start. Plan to succeed.

CHAPTER 6
THE BEST PLAN-PRELIMINARIES

The key to success when setting up your practice is to have a plan, a business plan designed for a professional practice. There are several reasons for preparing a business plan, as a blueprint to start up a business, as a tool to secure finance, as an ongoing management tool and as an operational guide for day-to-day practice. A good business plan will be capable of all of these purposes.

Most of the work and research for your business plan happens before you set up your practice; however, it is a work in progress, as is your practice. To be truly effective we should revisit and revise our plan at least annually. If any big changes occur, such as taking on staff, winning a large contract or changing focus of the practice, then a revision is in order. The best plan is an up-to-date plan. It is prudent to include the version number, date of the plan and note the author. Presenting this information in a footer is very practical and professional.

The initial decisions for your business are often the most significant. The front page of your plan includes such basic details as your trading name, your address, your phone number, your contact details (including web page and email), your ABN (Australian business number or the equivalent for where you practice) and your business logo.

These decisions define your business, now and forever. The name of your business along with your logo is its identity. All future transactions evolve from this marketing platform. We will create two new fictitious businesses and look at two example front pages.

1. John Smith Counselling
    7 Tree Street
    Suburbia
    PH: 0444 444 444
    Email: johnsmith@hotmail.com
    Web: www.johnsmith.com
    ABN: 9999 999 999 99

2. Connect Counselling Pty Ltd.
    Unit 2 4 Main St
    Business Centre
    PH: 09 9999 999
    Mobile: 0444 444 444
    Email: reception@connectcounselling.com
    Web: connect counselling.com
    ABN: 9999 999 999 99

These counsellors may well be equally qualified, be members of a professional association and both be good at their job. However, what they have presented here allows the consumer to make some assumptions, rightly or wrongly. If you were searching for a counsellor, which would you choose?

This would depend largely on who you are and what your needs are. John Smith seems like a friendly guy who operates from the suburbs, probably his home. This is very personal. This may well appeal to some people. The fact that he works from home, has not splurged on an email address and only uses a mobile phone number, may mean he charges less, as his overheads are lower.

Other people may interpret this differently. They may feel that his business implies that he is a single operator, set up at home, with no frills. This may seem unprofessional to some. Some single women may even not feel comfortable going into a man's home alone for safety reasons.

John Smith's information will certainly impact and influence potential clients. As would Marys' who has set up Connect Counselling Pty. Ltd. What could her information tell us? There is certainly a more formal feel to this information.

Mary has taken a more formal business approach to her business, which she has made a propriety limited company. Businesses can come in many forms, sole trader, like John, a partnership or as a company. There are definite benefits in each and when setting up it is important that we consciously decide what shape your business will take. It also has implications when you look at taxation options.

Connect Counselling Pty. Ltd. Is located in a business district, on what we may assume is a main road. This is a high profile business, located within consumers' work region. This has some benefits; clients can come straight from work for appointments; the address is easily found and probably a well-known street; there is probably designated parking.

This location may work for some; some may prefer a practice located within a medical cluster of businesses.

Many clients like a counselling practice which in quite anonymous and discreet from the street. Some clients need to be on a public transport route, which is more likely to happen, with greater regularity of service, in a business or medical precinct than a residential one.

Connect Counselling Pty. Ltd. also seems to have the structure of a professional office, a landline phone, an email through a reception desk and a business web page. Clearly, this is not a private home business.

While both these businesses will appeal to different people, they will also appeal to a different demographic of people. There is an obvious need for both of these alternatives and others, but each needs to be professional.

Other decisions at this point are the required paperwork side of the first page. We should consider whether our business name is registered. The benefit in this is that it makes the name exclusive, so we will not see three Connect Counselling Pty Ltd. businesses. There will be no confusion, especially online and you can then define the intellectual property of the practice.

Australian Business Number (ABN) or the equivalent for where you live is a government requirement for taxation purposes. It also speaks to the legitimacy of your practice. We quote these numbers on invoices and receipts to clients, as a matter of law. If you are reading this outside of Australia then please check the relevant registrations required by your government.

The final element of your front page is your business logo. Your logo is usually the first visual that people have of your practice. First impressions matter.

The dictionary meaning of a logo is a symbol, sign, or emblem. Human beings have used such symbols throughout time to convey a succinct message, making things easily recognizable. This is a tool you can use to build an identity for your business, as part of its trademark or brand, and to generate favourable thoughts and feelings about your practice.

A logo needs to be original and memorable for the greatest impact. A logo is a core identifier of a business, used on business cards, letterhead, and advertising material. More than a mere visual mark, it is the face of your business, and so it must be designed for the greatest impact. Ultimately, you want customers to connect your logo to your business and its values.

The design and development of a business logo is important. If you rush into preparing a logo, you may regret it and want to make a change down the road. The problem with this is that you can confuse customers and lose the advantages of having a logo.

When creating your logo, it is important to reflect the culture and values of your business. If these are still unclear, postpone the design of your logo until you have a clearer picture of your practice. Choosing colours, shapes, typefaces and pictures for your logo is a difficult process and needs consideration over time.

Colours express meanings and are associated with emotions. We all recognize red as the angry colour, and so would not choose this as a colour for a therapeutic practice's logo. It makes sense to select colours that will have the appropriate desired emotional affect. Similarly, the symbol or picture you chose should be appropriate to best describe your business.

When we think of the most recognizable logos, the logos of companies like Nike, Coke, Red Cross and Mc Donald's immediately come to mind. The reason for this is that they are simple, colour significant and emotionally connecting for most people.

Now you have completed all the requirements for a first page of your plan for your practice, you are well on your way to achieving a business identity. Congratulations!

❧

When you or other people look at your business plan, like all long documents, it is advisable to have a summary page. This enables the reader to get the general gist of the document. Although it appears at the beginning of the plan, we usually write the summary last, when we have completed all research and the business's profile is determined.

The summary provides an overview of your business. It shows what distinguishes your products or services from your competitors. It may include a statement about your business values and ethics along with your key objectives and any critical factors to the success of your business venture.

The summary generally is around a page and a half, and include a brief overview of the following items:

- your business;
- information about you and any partners etc.;
- your products and services, the benefits they provide, and who will be your clientele;
- your overall objectives and competitive advantage;
- the marketing strategy; and
- key figures from the financial forecasts.

We will revisit this information when we arrive at the end of the plan and look at an example.

CHAPTER 7
THE BEST PLAN-PURPOSE

The next part of your plan defines the business. This is achieved by creating a mission statement and setting business objectives for your practice. A mission statement is aimed at your customers and should sum up, in simple terms, what you do, how you do it and why.

Let's look at our two examples from Chapter 6, John Smith and Connect Counselling Pty. Ltd., and see what their mission statements may look like.

John Smith may have a mission statement that reads, 'Friendly, affordable, professional counselling'.

Connect Counselling Pty. Ltd. might have a mission statement that reads, 'Professional, confidential counselling for your whole family.' Both of these are good, valid mission statements that communicate to clients the values of each practice.

Your business objectives define what goals your business is aiming to achieve. Your objectives should be S.M.A.R.T. and include a mix of short and long-term goals.

Specific - Decide what you want. Your first step in any goal-setting framework must be to decide what it is you hope to achieve. At this stage, it's OK to start general. Whether your goal is long term or short term, most people start out with only a general idea of what they want. You move from the general to the specific by adding details and defining your terms.

For example, maybe your initial goal is to earn a living, knowing that will be your basis for creating a more specific goal.

Specific goals then give your general goals a much greater chance of being accomplished. To set a specific goal you must answer the six "W" questions:

*Who: Who is involved? Are you operating alone, have you a team, employees?
*What: What do you want to accomplish? Is this a certain number of clients, a set number of referral sources, a specific income or profit?
*Where: Identify a location.
*When: Establish time frames both long term and short term.
*Which: Determine which requirements and restraints will be part of the process. In other words, what will you need to do to achieve your goal? What obstacles will you face?
*Why: Specific reasons, purpose or benefits of accomplishing the goal. What does achieving these goals give you?

Measurable - Establish concrete criteria for measuring progress toward achieving each goal you set. When you measure your progress, you stay on track, reach your target dates, and experience the exhilaration of achievement that encourages the continued effort required to reach your goal. To determine if your goal is measurable, ask questions such as:

How much?
How many?
How will I know when it is accomplished?

Set up a system to measure your progress for each criterion you set. If your goal is, say, a certain profit, set up a regular Profit and Loss Statement to enable you to measure your achievement. If it is a certain number of clients a month, set up a client register to deliver this information.

Attainable - By identifying goals that are most important to you, you begin to work out ways you can make them come to fruition. You develop the attitudes, abilities, skills, and financial capacity to reach them. Previously overlooked opportunities bring you closer to the achievement of your goals.

Identify restraints and obstacles you may encounter and whether you'll be able to overcome them. To achieve any goal, you will face challenges so plan for them. The question to consider here is whether it's reasonable to think you'll be able to accomplish your goal in the face of these challenges.

Be realistic about the amount of time you have to devote to your goals as well as your personal background, knowledge, and any physical limitations. Think about your objective realistically; set a goal that is attainable for you with your life complexities at the present time.

Sometimes we have to consider the complexities of life into the future. I personally had to factor in my husband's plans for his business and also the events in my children's lives. For example, was I going to be flexible in my business hours to spend time with my grandchildren, to travel with my husband, to be home at meal times?

Assess your level of commitment. Even if a goal is theoretically achievable, you must be committed to making the efforts necessary to reach it. Ask yourself the following questions:

Are you prepared to make the necessary commitment to reach your target?

Are you willing to dramatically alter or at least adjust aspects of your life?

If not, is there a more achievable target you are willing to work for?

Your goal and your commitment level should match up. I have often supervised counsellors who want to make a living from full-time work as a counsellor. This is quite a commitment to make and many struggle to let go of their other employment and so stay in the part-time-practice mode of working. Often the financial certainty of the other job disables the commitment to full-time counselling. Their goal becomes unachievable.

Relevant - How well does your goal reflect your desires? Closely related to a goal's attainability is its relevance. If your goal is to make a million dollars in the first twelve months then this may well not be the vehicle for you! The question to ponder here is whether this goal will be fulfilling for you as an individual in your pursuit as a professional.

This is a moment to revisit the "why" question. Ask yourself if this goal will truly fulfil your desires or if there's a different goal that's more important to you. Consider your other goals and circumstances. It's also important to consider how your goal fits with other plans you have in life. Conflicting plans can create problems.

This was the case in point for the first counsellor I began teaching to take over my practice. We worked together, teaching and learning, with the same goal in mind—she would eventually take over the practice. This goal was in conflict with her family goal and when the family made a decision to leave the country, the goal of owning a practice was no longer relevant to her.

In other words, it's important to determine if your goal fits in with the rest of what is going on in your life. If it doesn't, this doesn't necessarily mean you need to abandon it altogether. Adjust your goal for relevance. If you decide your goal is relevant and will work well with your other plans, you can move on to the last step. If not, you'll need to make some more revisions.

When in doubt, go with what you're passionate about. A goal that you care deeply about will be both more relevant and achievable than one you're only sort of interested in. A goal that will fulfil your dreams will be much more motivating and worthwhile to you.

Timely - Set a time frame. This means your goal should have a deadline, or there should be a date set for completion, and regular revision.

Setting a timeline for your goal helps you identify and stick to the specific actions that you need to take to work towards that goal. It removes the "one day" quality that goals sometime attract, or, as Napoleon Hill put it, "A goal is a dream with a deadline." When you don't set a timeline, there is no internal pressure to accomplish the goal, so it can often end up being put on the back burner.

Setting benchmarks, especially if your goal is very long term, can be useful to break your goal up into smaller goals. This can help you measure your progress and make it manageable.

For example, if your goal is to have twenty appointments a week within one year, start with, the benchmark to sign up three new clients each week. This is less daunting and creates an incentive for consistent effort rather than a big push to find lots of clients during the first couple of months. And, if this turns out to be too much or too little for you, you can go back and revise the goal to make it more achievable.

Focus on the long term and the short term. Consistent progress toward your goals means keeping one eye on today and eye on the future. Within your established time frame, you might ask yourself:

What can I do today to reach my goal? If the goal is to find three new clients a week, one daily goal might be making two marketing phone calls each day.

In this section, it's a good idea to include your personal objectives, which should underpin your reasons for going into business. Our whole life goals, relationships and well-being all effect our business decisions. For example, if early retirement and travel is something you and your partner are planning, this effects the planning of your business, as do plans to have a family and your desired income levels. To plan a practice without considering all these factors would be unrealistic.

This is also where you outline your exit strategy for the business, which may include passing the business on to your children, seeking investors or partners or selling the practice to fund your retirement.

Consider how your exit strategy fits with your business and personal objectives. This one area is largely overlooked in practice planning. However, if you are setting up a successful practice then succession becomes very relevant. There is scope to mentor the future owner of your practice, take on partners to further establish and grow your practice and ultimately sell the practice or your own part of it. There is also the option of becoming a silent partner and living off dividends in retirement. In fact, this may be a goal from the start. The law profession has an extremely effective and efficient model for succession with its system of associates, partners and hierarchy.

When we revisit our two examples from Chapter 6, a succession plan may be difficult to imagine for John Smith; however, Connect Counselling Pty. Ltd. may well be a saleable asset and a succession plan would definitely be considered desirable.

To achieve this planning is essential. We need goals like when to employ someone for coaching to take over, when to cease taking on new clients and how long the transition will take.

The succession planning for your business becomes a whole of life financial planning strategy. If this is not one of your strengths, enlist a financial planner to your team.

❧

One very important decision you will make is the commencement date of your practice. This will help define some of your goals as far as timing is concerned. To commence your practice you will naturally have to have many things already in place—your office and your systems for banking, phones and the like. Your commencement date becomes the benchmark from which you work back. For example, if you set July first as your start date, knowing that phone companies can take up to a month to deliver their services, you can begin this process as early as required.

My commencement date was well organized. My office was set up; my business cards and letterheads were printed; I had designed my receipts and invoices; my tools of the trade were all prepared and I felt ready. I had begun advertising and had actually run a couple of free workshops, which brought me clients. I was working as a counsellor from day one of my practice. This gave me confidence and I felt like a counsellor. I was a counsellor, not just qualified as one.

Often I hear from the counsellors who I supervise that the constant struggle to establish themselves in their practices and get clients saps their confidence as counsellors. Being unprepared or disorganized can cause you not to work at your best. Prior planning and preparation prevents poor performance.

Before opening the doors of your practice financial decisions need to be made. What exactly is your starting point? What capital are you putting into the practice to begin with? What assets will you need to begin with? Where is this money coming from? Prioritize the needs of the business. Some purchases can wait until your practice is profit making, things like decorations and ornaments.

List the capital the business started with and specify the amount provided by you. If monies were borrowed to start the business, state the amount borrowed and from who.

Another starting decision that we need to make is which legal structure the business operates under: i.e. sole trader, partnership, company or trust. This depends largely on how you envision your practice in the future, and if the rationale behind this decision is outside your scope of knowledge, seek advice from an accountant. Do this before you begin as it can take a couple of weeks to organize, depending on your decision.

The laws relating to taxation accounting for differing legal structures are complicated. Some accountants will recommend the use of a trust. The distribution of your profits can become a complicated process and if you are not engaging an accountant, and don't have hour upon hour to track the changes in taxation law, then a simpler legal structure of practice may suit better.

You may also wish to include any plans for a change in structure down the track – i.e. from sole trader to company

– depending on the level of business growth you're expecting to see over time. Change can be easily achieved if you plan for it and do the necessary research beforehand.

This was a decision I made with my practice, on the advice of my accountant. After a couple of years practicing as a sole trader, which is inexpensive to set up, I changed my practice to a proprietary limited company. As my business had grown there were benefits in becoming a company that did not exist in the early days. I did have to rely on the expertise of my accountant on when and how to make this decision. As I became busier in the practice, I had less time to research such things and could not possibly keep my finger on the pulse enough to know when the best time to make this change was.

CHAPTER 8
THE BEST PLAN-PRODUCTS

Let's start looking now at exactly what your practice will be. It's time to work on a concise description of the practice including what modalities, services and products it provides to what type of market.

Your study, interests and personal experience will usually determine what field or fields you will prefer to work in. Setting up in a niche market can have many advantages. Finding a niche market that fits with your area of interest can be difficult, unless you have a specific concept you wish to pursue. For example, setting up as a counsellor who works with children is a market that exists. Setting up as a counsellor for children who suffer from anxiety is more specific and enables you to 'become an expert' in this field over time.

Niche markets can be limiting and, often, when setting up your practice, a more general approach may be easier. Marketing for a niche market, while tricky, can be more cost effective than competing in the general market. Careful consideration of whether a niche market suits you, the current market and the competition, can make the decision of whether to aim for a niche or not easier.

If you have trouble deciding which services you want to provide, maybe start with those you do not want to provide. For me, there was no interest in drug and alcohol counselling, and this was an area I always referred on. I felt this clashed with my desire and objective to work with families and children. I did not want a drug addict sharing my waiting room with children.

In deciding which areas you want your practice to focus on, look at the competitive advantage you will hold if you go down a certain road.

This is where you explore and research the uniqueness of your product or service, why there is a need or demand for it and what benefits it offers the customer. My focus on children and families was a unique proposition in the southern suburbs. There was a demand, because other services offered were centrally located in the city and the expanding suburbs meant a demand for local services. The benefit of being local was very appealing to busy families.

There were no other services offered by competitors in the area. I also had the advantage of my large workshopping room to hold workshops and seminars. Parenting workshops were a large part of the practice and a source of ongoing clientele.

While there were many counselling services in the area, my target market of children and families gave me a marketing edge. It was specific enough to enable advertising of services different to my competitors.

Did this limit my practice to only working with children and families? No. This naturally grew to include relationship counselling, grief counselling and work with anxiety and depression. As I explained in Chapter 1, I also had opportunities arise in pet grief and compassion fatigue. I also worked with Employee Assistance Programs. One of my original goals when I set up my practice was to include variety in my work. So, while I marketed to a niche market, I worked in a broad range of fields.

Your business plan is also a document where you can explore your own profile as a counsellor and practice owner.

This may be as simple as including your resume or may indeed be the place where you plan your resume. Provide an overview of your expertise along with any special skills, industry knowledge and experience you bring to the practice. Include any formal qualifications along with specific training you've undertaken or plan to undertake in the future. Highlight any prior successes you've had in running a business or in this particular field.

Remember this is a plan so it is also advisable to plan your future development as a professional here. If there are areas of interest you wish to develop then research, explore and set goals. Part of my plan has always been to travel interstate to a conference every second year. This enables me to access some good professional development and to network with some interesting professionals. I have attended some fabulous workshops in small groups at some of these conferences and learnt some fantastic strategies. Some of the people I have met at these conferences have also become friends and mentors.

Large conferences are certainly an opportunity and I am often puzzled that more counsellors don't take full advantage of them. I can only assume that counsellors do not plan for them and therefore are overwhelmed at the thought of travelling and paying for great professional development. I made this a "must have" in my budget.

This is also a great place to record all the professional development you have completed, the associations with which you are registered, and the insurances you have for yourself and your practice.

Let's take a close look now at the marketing aspect of your business plan. To devise a marketing plan the first thing we analyze and describe is exactly what products and services are being offered by your practice and what part they will play in the total profit and organization of your business.

Here is a simple example of this product range analysis. It shows what percentage of sales and profit each activity will contribute. This will help us to estimate revenues and returns later in the business plan. These are obviously estimates and depend largely on our objectives in the practice.

Product	% of total sales	% of total gross profit
General Counselling	30	22
Counselling for Children	35	34
Workshop 1	25	40
Workshop 2	10	4

Diagram 2

Once we have established what we are selling in our practice we can make a comparison and analyse our competition. Are your competitors offering the same services? What exactly are your competitors doing? How many are there? Is the market large enough to support all of you? What is your advantage over your competitors? Why will clients chose you?

Compare the features, benefits and advantages of your product or services over your competitors' offerings of the same, similar or substitute services.

Use the following table as an example to compare the attributes of your business with your significant competitors.

Business Feature	Your Business	Competitor 1	Competitor 2	Competitor 3
Counselling for children	Specialising in children	No mention of child counselling	Lists child counselling as service No. 7	No mention of child counselling
In an industrial setting	Available for EAPs	At home practice; no mention of EAPs	In medical centre; no mention of EAPs	Specialises in EAPs

Diagram 3

I found the easiest way to compare with competitors was to check out their web pages and see what services they offered. There is some benefit, however, to making a phone call and asking about a competitor's services as web pages are often static and services change over time. This became an issue for me when I looked at setting up a workshop for anxiety. None of my competitors seemed to be offering such a workshop but, as I soon found, one competitor had progressed and not updated their website. My program was compared often to the competitor's and, though I was confident in my material, clients who tried both courses were astounded at the different content and approach to the same issue. While I feel this worked to my advantage, the competitor was not happy and communicated this to me.

This is a great time to do a SWOT analysis to identify internal and external factors that may affect your business in a positive or negative way. Internal factors are strengths and weaknesses and external factors are opportunities or threats.

By understanding the strengths, weaknesses, opportunities and threats involved in your business, it becomes clearer to see what your competitive advantage is in the market. In the above example, the threat of government funding free services rarely affects niche markets. So offering niche services becomes a real advantage and this is where the focus of the business would go.

Strength (e.g.): Internal	Weakness (e.g.): Internal
<ul><li>Niche market</li><li>Excellent practice location</li><li>A variety of services</li></ul>	<ul><li>Little knowledge of accounting</li><li>Limited to one person</li><li>Inexperience</li></ul>
Opportunity (e.g.): External	**Threat (e.g.): External**
<ul><li>Entering a growing need for services</li><li>Greater public recognition of mental health</li><li>Acquiring distribution rights for a complementary product</li></ul>	<ul><li>New competitor entering your market</li><li>New regulations</li><li>More government funding to provide free services</li></ul>

Diagram 4

We saw this recently in Australia with the introduction by the government of subsidised pre-marital counselling. This would not affect those in a general practice but for a private practice linked to a marriage celebrant, this new incentive could make or break a practice. The sudden withdrawal of this funding also had its effects on some practices.

There is a need for counsellors to be aware of this government, and even other local agency incentives as they can really impact a practice. There are often local agency incentives that are not advertised that can affect your practice. For quite a while, one of our local agencies offered a $200 rebate on training related to running a business. This was not widely advertised and many practitioners were unaware. Such funding for business development can be hugely advantageous for a small practice. This is why and where research is so valuable.

Understanding your competitive advantage gives you the basis of your marketing strategy. If your practice is multifaceted then it may also be beneficial to segment your market analysis into separate markets. Marketing is different, for example, we would not target families with the same marketing we would use to engage businesses with EAPs. Although all of your customers use your product or service, they will value different aspects of it such as price, presentation format or ease of access. You can segment your market by customers that have shared values.

For example, if your practice focuses on grief counselling, you may well market differently for loss of a loved one compared to the grief at the loss of a pet, a relationship or a job.

By understanding the needs of each segment, you can tailor your marketing mix to deliver what your customer values and needs. Each segment will offer growth and profit opportunities so the trick is to deliver the best offer to the best segment.

You can profile your target market/segments using four categories:

Geographic: e.g. location, population size or climate
Demographic: e.g. age, gender, family size, family life cycle or income

Psychographic: e.g. social class, lifestyle, motivation or personality

Behavioural: e.g. short-term vs. long-term therapy, one-on-one vs. group vs. Workshop

For example, to run a workshop targeting children suffering from anxiety you would market geographically to schools, children's activity centres, day care centres etc. in an area where young families live. There would be age considerations such as six to twelve-year-olds. Unless the workshop is free, there has to be some economic consideration of the advertising; lifestyle may also dictate the best time for a workshop such as this as many children are involved in afterschool and weekend sport.

When we profile a workshop segment of our practice, as you can see, it is not as simple as advertising as you would advertise your practice generally.

Another strategy for defining your services is the concept of add-ons. These come in many forms from relaxation CDs to podcasts to group meditation sessions, parenting groups and mini yoga workshops for children. The list is long and unlimited. These add-ons usually only require in-practice advertising to existing clients and, though they may take a little organisation initially, once they are developed they become simple to integrate into your practice.

One real benefit of add-ons is that during busy times, you can shelve them and then unpack them when needed. I found also that these add-ons are a simple word of mouth advertisement and many a new client came from attending an add-on activity and then becoming a counselling client.

CHAPTER 9
THE BEST PLAN-PRICE

One of the most difficult decisions many counsellors say they have to make is how much to charge for services provided. To develop a price strategy it is essential to consider the market value of the services by comparing to the existing services of our competitors. It is also important to compare apples to apples, so in our original examples of John Smith and Connect Counselling it could be argued reasonably that the two practices offer different services, or at least different environments and perhaps different levels of professionalism. The fact that John Smith works from home means maybe he can provide an economic price. This also depends on the value that clients place on the services provided, not just the value the practice owners place.

That being said another consideration is about the revenue required to break even and pay the wages of the employees of the practice. Clearly, a one-man show could not afford a receptionist, but if the practice is one that plans to grow then these costs are worth considering. Note the difference between total hours worked and chargeable hours available. Chargeable hours are the face-to-face hours for which you charge your hourly rate. Total hours include research, note writing and administration time.

Calculation of charge out rate for a one-person practice might be calculated like this:

Item		$; weeks; hours
Annual profit required		$
Add annual running costs		$
Total revenue required	(a)	$
Weeks worked per year		weeks
Hours worked per week		hours
Total hours worked (100%)		hours
Chargeable hours available (%)	(b)	hours
Hourly charge out rate (revenue required divided by chargeable hours)	(a) (b)	$
Hourly charge out rate including GST	=	$

Diagram 5

All practices must cover some costs such as insurance and Association fees. We all also desire to be paid our worth for the hours we put in. While working out an hourly rate to charge clients for their sessions, it is important to factor in the time we spend writing up notes and researching for our clients. There are also similar costs to consider when charging for workshops, such as the hours we take to write and prepare them.

The mentality from some counsellors dictates keeping our prices as low as possible for our clients who clearly have concerns and issues to begin with. The thought of adding to these woes can lead some counsellors to undervalue what they do in their work. One counsellor I supervised decided that her client's grief was so intense she felt she could only charge $10 per session so as not to further upset the client. Her work has more value than this.

Please, I am not saying there is no room for charity, pro bono work or even discounts but we need to plan these as well. My practice's plan had allowances for free work with a not-for-profit organization and discounts to clients through a program run by local government.

Many counsellors question the payment for non-sessional services such as writing letters, answering subpoenas, preparation of a client's copy of their file. I have decided this issue on a client-by-client basis. I have a structure of fees for these services already calculated, and, depending on the circumstances, these may vary. A good example of this was on the day I received two emails from lawyers representing clients of mine in court, one for the husband and one for the wife. I was more than happy to provide a summary of their sessions to their respective lawyers. One email was demanding, questioned my competence and wanted the report "immediately". The other lawyer presented a professional looking form, was polite and respectful. I did them both "immediately" but charged more for the lawyer who put me under pressure. I value professionalism in other professions too. Unfortunately, the client probably paid the price for this lawyer's lack of professionalism.

Some counsellors also seem to stumble with how to charge if during the initial session we decide to refer to another counsellor or other professional. I decide this on the criterion of "Did I serve the client?" If it is apparent early in the session that I cannot help a client, I am not going to charge them for simply telling them I cannot help them. If, however, I have completed a session and then we have agreed that another professional may be a better choice, then, yes, I will charge. Sometimes this is not so clear and I will decide on a reduced fee.

Another faux pas I find counsellors fall into is, "I'm not experienced yet so I will start pricing low and increase my prices as I get more experience." You cannot be almost a counsellor or a little bit of a counsellor. This is unprofessional. If you are setting yourself up in a practice, you are a counsellor and you will be doing counselling. Your pricing should reflect this.

There is a sensitivity to increasing prices in any field, but in counselling we are talking about clients with whom we work hard at building rapport and a professional relationship. If we regularly increase our prices, what effect does this have on the therapeutic relationship we have developed? We cannot continually put that trust to the test.

Does having a great reputation and getting most clients through referral rather than advertising mean you can charge more? Wealth of experience and becoming "expert" is achieved over years and your prices should reflect this. If you are in a niche market and are an expert who has put in the hard yards to gain knowledge, why should you not be compensated for this? There is value, quality and prestige earned when you become a specialist.

Naturally, your prices should reflect the quality of your products and services. Strategies are also needed to define and improve your services. So at what level of quality are your services? Do you have good resources for clients to take home and read? Is your administration professional with invoices and receipts for clients? Do your clients leave your office feeling that you have met their needs? Are your workshops delivering the promised results?

The only real measure of these questions is client feedback. This can come directly from a feedback sheet at workshops or through feedback at different stages of your work with clients. Certainly, a feedback form when you are finishing up with a client will be beneficial in understanding the client's experience with your practice.

This is critical when first setting up your practice as you are travelling in uncharted water and feedback is a simple tool for improving your services. As you become more experienced, you may find it easier to ask for verbal feedback from clients as part of their own progress check-in. Simply asking if a strategy has been successful for a client informs you about your client but also about your strategy. If a client, for example, tells you they found the strategy difficult to implement, maybe you need a take home resource explaining it clearly for future clients. The ultimate feedback is referral. You can rest easy knowing that you are effective if past clients regularly refer your services.

Feedback is valuable only if the information gained is acted upon. Over time, many a file of feedback sheets has sat unanalysed in filing cabinets. I have been guilty of the quick glance and file attitude myself, but when you take the time to analyse the feedback properly, you can initiate change to improve your services. Then maybe a price rise can be justified.

CHAPTER 10

THE BEST PLAN-PLACE

The location, environment and atmosphere of your practice will have a profound impact on its success. It is important to develop an environment that reflects the goals and ethos of your practice. This environment depends on who you are and what you wish your practice to reflect. It also depends on the modalities you choose for your practice. For example, if you were to open a practice specialising in executive stress and business practices, you would surely want your practice located in the heart of a business district. However, if your practice focusses specifically on children then a business district may not be as suitable as a suburban location. If your practice is dealing with drug addiction, is a home office the best, safest environment?

It is also important to consider the existing services in the area. Too many family counsellors in one area may limit the demand for your services. However, setting up a family counselling practice in the same centre as a family doctor and child psychologist may increase your market share and allow referral agreements to exist.

I have actually supervised a counsellor who targeted their practice for FIFO (Fly-in-fly-out) families, setting her practice up in an inner city office. Her logic was that this was central; families from all areas would come to her practice and public transport into the city centre was excellent. Unfortunately, her practice did not thrive.

When we looked at the demographic of FIFO families, they mostly lived in the new, outer lying suburbs. When we did an online survey, we found these sometimes-single parents very rarely travelled to the city. Having children made this difficult, despite public transport; they wanted their services locally situated.

Despite this example, the consideration of public transport can be significant, especially in low socio-economic areas.

So where did this counsellor go wrong? There was no profiling of her potential clientele. The often-young FIFO spouse is a very busy person. Many of these spouses work and fitting appointments in is difficult even without having to travel to a centrally located office. How can their needs best be met? Also consider, when the income earner is home, what is most convenient for them?

This counsellor was also offering one-on-one counselling when possibly a group approach may have attracted more clients, especially for the spouses. This could also be the beginnings of the support network these women rely on so heavily. No one understands like someone experiencing the same lifestyle as you. The issues of the men and women working FIFO are common and shared by most FIFO workers and maybe even a men's group would be helpful. There is also an argument for couples groups as well.

Understanding the needs of your specific client base is certainly important, and becomes more important the more specialised you become. The research involved in profiling a client base is quite extensive and time consuming, but worth the trouble in the end.

Once the location of the practice is established, the next priority is to set up a therapeutic environment within your counselling rooms. There needs to be a balance between a professional business office and a welcoming, comfortable setting that allows and encourages your clients to talk. Depending on the client base, this can vary from practice to practice; a setting, room and environment for family counselling, for example, would differ from that for grief counselling or a group session.

What your rooms look like very much depends on the work you plan to do. If part of your plan is to do seminars and workshops then you will have to cater for this in your setup or identify available rooms you may be able to hire.

Over the years I had many clients comment on how inviting and relaxing my consulting room was. I have also heard from many of my clients disturbing disaster stories of counsellors' living rooms, hired by the hour, cold, sterile offices and even stories of counselling sessions taking place in a café because a shared office had been double booked. To be treated as professionals we need to present a professional environment.

Quiet, air-conditioned and comfortable rooms are the bare minimum requirement. The provision of tissues and glasses of water is also presumed. The provision of a waste paper bin for those tissues is often overlooked. Minor details, I know, but things that make for uncomfortable moments for clients. Sometimes this makes a marked difference to the success of a session.

The lighting in a room also has an effect on clients. Natural light is more relaxing than artificial lights, especially florescent lights. If you have florescent lighting, it may be a good idea to put diffusers over them to soften the light or use standard lamps instead. When a client is upset and crying, these stark lights can make them feel more vulnerable.

We should also give thought to the colour scheme and textures in the consulting room. Calm, peaceful colours such as blues and greens and soft textures will make your clients feel more relaxed.

My office always afforded extras on top of the basics. It is amazing how teenagers feel free to talk while they pop the wrapper on a Mentos. Clients are much more expressive if they have pencil and paper to doodle with while they talk and people of all ages and genders tend to pick up the teddy on the side of the chair and play or cuddle with it while they talk.

Attention to detail in the waiting room is also important. I noticed over a few months that the monthly women's magazines in the waiting room were untouched, but the health magazine was well read. This told me something about my clientele—they were interested in health not gossip. I adjusted the reading in the waiting room to reflect this.

I also had many people comment on the photographs on the wall of tranquil ocean scenes. More than one client told me they always felt calm when they came to my offices. It was nothing I was doing. I had merely created the right environment.

The flip side of this calming environment is the efficient, effective business side. The reception desk was a clear boundary for clients. The choice of payment via cash, EFTPOS, credit card or direct debit made things seamless for the client. I even progressed in the last few months to mobile phone transfers. The professional invoice/receipt available to clients at the time of payment was welcomed by some and not required by others but always offered.

There was also an ever-changing stream of information for clients, both in the waiting room and at reception. Some of this was purely advertising for a workshop or seminar but I also had copies of articles available for those clients who were interested. Some clients looked forward to seeing what the latest information sheet in the waiting room was offering. Clients took many of these sheets home.

While focusing on the environment, it is also important to consider the web page for your practice. This should also be an inviting, reassuring experience for clients. To be effective, web pages must be easy to use and encourage further contact without being pushy. We will be looking at web page set up in detail a bit later but please remember it is a part of your environment that should be welcoming.

If a client sees a peaceful, comforting web page and books an appointment only to find a stark office when they arrive they will feel distrust. All parts of the working environment should feel congruent for the client.

It is also important that your website target the market your business wants to attract geographically. A general counselling practice in the suburbs really won't be attractive to someone who lives on the opposite side of the city. If you don't target your location you may well spend valuable time talking to and referring clients to other counsellors because of your location.

If you have a specialist practice, however, you will need to cast a wide net and set up your web page for this purpose. This is part of optimising your web page and if this is not a strength for you, you may need to add an information technology (IT) specialist to your team.

CHAPTER 11
THE BEST PLAN-PROMOTION

When looking at your promotional strategy, which will ensure that clients find out about your services, the obvious tool we use is advertising. Depending on your practice, and what you hope it achieves, you have many options for advertising. Some businesses may get results from advertising in local newspapers, some by letterbox drops and some by posters on community pin boards. I myself had success with a letterbox drop in an industrial estate seeking EAP clients. However, I would not use this form of advertising to attract general counselling clients. The advertising strategy you use depends largely on who your target market is.

I found in my practice the most efficient way to advertise was via my webpage and social media. In our high tech world, I felt it unnecessary to do hard copy advertising so put my resources into the development of an optimised webpage.

There are some advantages to this. Although the setup costs are high and webpages need monitoring, there is little need to rehash the advertising regularly. The return on this investment was much higher than on any other advertising investment I undertook. I am not a very tech savvy person and so relied on an expert to develop my advertising. Whether you do your page yourself or have someone do it for you, it is important to have a webpage that reflects you and your practice. It should use colours that are therapeutic, font to match and appropriate pictures. If you are a counsellor who likes to share information, this is also the perfect platform for this.

I have spoken with many counsellors who have constructed webpages and get little or no return on their investment. A good, optimised webpage is crucial. Just having a page is good to refer clients to for extra information but if you want to use your webpage as advertising then it must be optimised to get results.

Social media, if handled professionally can be a great advertising tool. It is, however, important that you keep your personal life separate from your professional life. Photos of family, holidays, pets and what you ate for dinner have no place on a professional page.

The next best advertising platform for me was definitely word of mouth. Referral by client is the ultimate in reputation and therefore in public relations. To have the name of your practice recognised and attract new clients is confidence building and is free advertising. As I shared in Chapter One, my first client from referral happened twenty-one days after I opened. This was not just luck. I was very proactive in the early days, making sure all clients left my practice every session with at least two pieces of paper with my contact information. One of these was my business card with their next appointment filled in on the back, the other a fact sheet, an article to read or sometimes some homework to be completed. On all of these, my company logo was prominent as was my phone number.

One of my most successful referrals came from a child client. I had, as an activity while we were working, given the child some bookmarks to colour in. They had great little sayings on them like "Smiles are free" and "Be the best you that you can be." My client coloured in frantically while we talked. At the end of the session, we laminated the bookmarks that all had my logo and phone number on the back. Eight bookmarks went home that day and some were shared with friends. Three of these friends also became my clients. Quite obviously, conversations had happened with the parents of these children and a reputation was formed.

I could have achieved the same result in that session by having the client draw pictures on blank pieces of paper that could have gone home and been shared with friends. Maybe the parents would have talked anyway, I do not know for sure. What I do know is that each of those parents had my phone number handy. Advertising mission accomplished!

Over time, I realised that a lot of advertising is opportunistic. As a client leaves and speaks of going to see a friend who has recently lost their dog, an opportunity arises to share a pet grief booklet full of information, which also sports, you guessed it, the practice logo and phone number. These opportunities have been fruitful for me over the time of my business and when analysing the data collected on client intake forms about how the client found my practice, through a friend is a common comment, second only to via my webpage.

Sometimes advertising through your webpage is not enough. I found this to be true when I wanted to advertise workshops. Although all the information and enrolment details are on the webpage, such events not held regularly or often, need special attention. Sometimes this was as simple as advertising in the reception area of the practice but sometimes there was a need for more targeted advertising. A great example of this was our parenting workshop that we held every couple of months. In-house advertising would usually engage a couple of attendees but we would target a couple of school newsletters as well to increase the number of clients.

Building a public image for your practice is also important. The smallest things like answering the phone rather than letting it go through to a message, the way you answer the phone and having the right message when you can't answer the phone are minor details that have a big impact. I once rang a counsellor with the intention of referring a client. The phone was answered by the counsellor's husband with a grunted greeting. When I asked if I had the right number for the counsellor, I was told yes but she was in the toilet, could I ring back? Needless to say, I referred to a different counsellor. This counsellor may well have been the right person for my client but I do not like referring to counsellors who are not professional. The professionalism of my referrals reflects on me too. Had I been a client, what picture would I have of this counsellor in my head? How confident would I be in a face-to-face meeting?

Many counsellors have told me that they have trouble converting phone calls into clients. On investigation, I usually find that some counsellors try to start solving on the phone. Unless you are going to spend a lot of time on the phone with the client, I think this is counter-productive and even careless and can lead to misunderstanding. I find that, if we use our listening skills then assure the person that you are ready to listen and look for strategies in the first session, the client will commit to the first session. Give the client lots of information, your fee, payment options, your address, parking, and your webpage address so they can see what you are all about. When the client feels you have given them something, they will be more likely to engage. This can be achieved by simply giving them the opportunity to ask questions and give them answers. It is important at this stage to be in the role of receptionist rather than counsellor. Give the sort of information a receptionist gives and leave the counselling for in the session.

Public relations can be the smallest of things. The difference between the first impression made by the counsellor who searches around in their wallet and produces a dog-eared business card and the one who instantly produces a clean, crisp card is enormous. It is true, each client is different, but I am confident most would prefer the second business card when looking for a professional counsellor.

Engaging with people in the local community can also be a rewarding public relations exercise. A forty-minute chat at a new parent night at a primary school on developing a good relationship with the school, a handout with your logo and phone number can lead to ongoing work. Sure, you have to put in time talking with the teachers and writing your talk but for the couple of hours this takes, one parent or child as a new client can lead to many hours of billable time. This does not take into account the possibility of clients just because they now know their local counsellor and have their phone number on hand.

This has also built a relationship with the school and, in the future, if they have a family who need help, they know your name; they know you are prepared to work with children, parents and families. Leave some business cards. The same principles apply to any setting, such as giving a talk at a FIFO head office of talking to vets about compassion fatigue.

There are many avenues to investigate in the pursuit of clients, but each one can be an opportunity to network in your community, whether with schools, businesses, clubs or associations, and each is a public relations operation.

CHAPTER 12
THE BEST PLAN-PEOPLE

If you expect to be a great counsellor, a great business owner, and to do it all on your own, you are going to be very busy! And probably very disappointed! At this point, we need to be very realistic and recognise the limitations of our knowledge and skills.

Do you know the most effective and fruitful way to account for taxation? Do you understand the effects and side effects of anti-depressants? Are you a guru of all things I.T.? What about the intricacies of family law?

We cannot expect to be able to do all of these things for ourselves. If we engage experts to handle these areas it allows us to focus on what we do best—counselling. Sure, being totally naïve about these things is not healthy, but to learn gradually while being guided by an expert is a productive and progressive way forward.

When I first set up my practice, my area of least knowledge was I.T. Sure, I was competent in writing a word document; I could put together a mean PowerPoint presentation and at a pinch could work formulas in Excel spreadsheets. But where to start when I needed a web page? Not just any web page, one that would reflect my business ethos, one that would attract traffic and one that would meet the needs of my clients. This was way too much for me. I needed to engage someone to work with me on this.

The research continued. How do you find a team member who will work well with you, hear what you say, and share their knowledge? I was very lucky in my search here. I found a young, experienced and enthusiastic web designer who was interested in what I was asking. This piece of my puzzle unfolded effortlessly and I loved being on a different learning curve for a while.

As time progressed, I was glad to have such great IT support. With all the new technology, changes in social media and the popularity of mobile devices, I would never have coped on my own. After a two-year association, I was devastated to hear my IT guy wanted a change in career and my search began all over again. This time, however, I knew exactly what I needed and how to talk the talk to get it. Once again, I was fortunate in making a good connection.

Although I have a background in accounting, I did not want my time in the business consumed with bookwork. For years, I had been doing my husband's business books in an electronic accounting package. This is a simple, time efficient package, so I decided to stick with it. I had a great working relationship with my husband's accountant, so using her for my business was an easy decision. We understood each other and could have a laugh on the phone, usually at our business experiences.

If I had not been so lucky, this would have meant another search. I really believe, when looking for support for your business, one of the best ways to find good people is via word of mouth. There is a lot to be said, however, for finding a registered professional who is up with all the latest taxation changes. It can save you money and much angst.

This part of your practice's plan is the who's who of your practice and is definitely not set in concrete. These details should be updated at regular intervals and should be checked for currency regularly.

As you have probably recognised by now, there is a lot of thought and decision making to be done to complete a comprehensive business plan for your practice. There are some major benefits to spending the time to do this, however. I recently spoke with a counsellor who, when seeing a client, needed to refer to an expert. He had not researched his referral list properly and referred to a psychiatrist who had left the country. When the upset client had called back and been rather abusive over the phone, the counsellor had wanted to contact me, his supervisor, to have a chat. He had lost my business card and had gotten himself in a state looking for my details online.

When I spoke to him, my message was simple, plan for everything. If you have one comprehensive document with all these details in then life becomes simple and even easy. Keeping this document up to date is also important and regular revisions are advised. Scheduling time every three months to revise and update should be considered.

As one of my passions is family counselling, I needed to find a family lawyer who I could work with. The benefits to both the lawyer and myself were immeasurable over time. A friend's son had set up as a family lawyer several years before I set up my business. When I contacted him to see if we could mutually refer, he was very cooperative. We established a fantastic working relationship where we both referred to the other and on occasion shared professional advice about cases.

This relationship was also profitable for me because when the law firm expanded and criminal lawyers were employed, a diversity of work came my way. I loved the variety of work. My days were always interesting and I never knew what each new day would bring.

My own doctor was an obvious choice to target as a team member as well. However, due mainly to the geographical location of our businesses, I targeted a couple of the doctors' surgeries close to my business as well. While I really had mixed results, one particular surgery was happy to form an alliance and became a regular referral source for me.

The greatest challenge for me was trying to set up a working relationship with other mental health professionals. This was partly due, I think, to the fact that I had been led to believe other professionals didn't respect counsellors. I felt I went cap in hand to discuss the concepts of mutual referral and cooperation. I soon learnt this was a mistake.

After several unsuccessful attempts, I reviewed my approach. I decided to use a 'what I can do for you' approach rather than the 'please refer to me' approach. The difference was amazing. The psychologist, child psychologist and the sex therapist I approached with the revised mentality all came on board as cooperative professionals with whom I have had a lasting working relationship.

In the interest of professionalism, having the right referral for the right client is imperative. When a client knows you need to send them to a specialist, and they see you have a solid relationship with that specialist, it gives the client confidence in both you and the specialist involved.

All of these relationships took time and definitely needed nurturing. However, the benefits, financially, in expanding my knowledge and in being able to serve my clients well, certainly outweighed the time and energy I injected into accomplishing these relationships.

At this point, it may be prudent to find a suitable supervisor, one who has set up a successful practice and who can guide you through the process. Remember your supervisor is a qualified counsellor too and is able to help you with personal issues pertaining to your practice. This is possibly one of the most important professional alliances you will have in your practice so do not be afraid to try more than one supervisor. There are no rules that say you must only have one supervisor and never change. It can be very therapeutic for your practice to have a variety of supervision.

The final set of team members, and by no means the most insignificant, is the network of counsellors I have worked with, referred to, shared knowledge with and bounced ideas off. I have worked with other counsellors to co-write programs and to co-facilitate workshops. These like-minded professionals have played an important role in my practice and I can only hope have also benefitted from our alliance. At one point, I was running tool-shed workshops where counsellors came together and shared strategies that they had found useful in their practices. This was sharing on a new level and we all learned many new concepts and strategies to use with our clients.

Spending time to develop relationships and form a cooperative and cohesive team has had a large impact on my practice. Many counsellors I have supervised are isolated and insular, and struggle to simply put together a referral list, let alone form alliances.

These relationships are important to the longevity of your practice; having a regular flow of clients from a variety of sources ensures a continuing turnover. This makes your practice marketable.

CHAPTER 13
THE BEST PLAN-PROCESSES

The processes you employ in your practice are the engine room of your business. The process of planning your business is one of the most important, as we have seen, but there are many others to be considered.

The development of your paperwork, including, of course, the company logo, is an integral part of your setup. Having the right forms on hand to write a referral, to release notes, for feedback forms, with bank details for electronic payment, intake and exit forms, client confidentiality and counsellor code of conduct forms, information fliers, reading for clients and brochures detailing your services makes the experience for both client and counsellor easier.

Information sheets and booklets were common handouts that I gave clients to take home. Over time, I developed many of these on varying topics and they were always well received by my clients. The fact that they physically had something to take home was a huge positive for some clients. Some would also browse my shelf on their way out and take home extras.

I would suggest, to start with, that developing common complaint information sheets for concerns such as sleep, relaxation and work life balance would be the logical first step. My sleep information included things like setting up daily routines that enable sleep, making bedrooms sleep friendly and a sensory meditation for night times. I must have handed out hundreds of these over time. I had a new client come into my practice once for some post-divorce help. As we spoke, she told me the only issue she had solved for herself was her lack of sleep. When I asked her how she had done this, she reached into her handbag and produced one of my sleep handouts. A friend had passed it on to her and she had not realised it was from my practice. She did, however, say when she googled for help she had recognised my practice name "from somewhere".

I also developed a separate set of forms for my child clients including a parent consent and confidentiality form, a child's confidentiality form, homework sheets and behaviour contracts. I developed these in a language easily comprehended by a child. Having children signing forms for themselves was an empowering strategy.

One of the most important pieces of paperwork you will develop is your business card. It is important that business cards are both professional and informative. I found it most beneficial to have a place for appointments on the reverse side of the business card. This meant my clients always had my contact details in their wallet and always had a written reminder of their appointment time.

Another process that I was often grateful that I set up from the very beginning was my report writing. Client files are the backbone of your business, especially as you get more clients, and need to be professionally maintained. Setting up professional files for clients, with intake forms with appropriate data fields and information, makes a practice flow easier. Properly prepared files mean there is no chance of forgetting details or losing information. These files become a collection point and referral place when you are preparing for a session. This can be critical, and if your notes are subpoenaed, they should be professional and accurate. I have supervised a counsellor who had notes subpoenaed in a separation case. They had decided early in the sessions with the clients that the same information was being regurgitated and they had stopped taking notes. This made it difficult to remember some of the details and made the counsellor look very unprofessional. This is another service we provide to clients and maintaining that professionalism is crucial to the integrity of the profession.

If you are conducting workshops as part of your practice, this introduces a completely new and different set of paperwork, from enrolment forms to handouts or workbooks and feedback forms. Many workshops also benefit from the use of the information sheets you have already prepared. For a long time I ran a workshop for veterinarians on compassion fatigue. One of the main issues these stressed vets suffered from was poor sleep. As such, I always had my sleep information sheets in my bag and usually every participant went away with a copy. This was beneficial to them in the first instance but was also a source of advertising for the practice.

It can be overwhelming when beginning a practice to try to produce all the required paperwork. It becomes a matter of prioritising the essential paperwork first and developing the optional extras as time permits. One area that is essential to have ready is your invoices and receipts.

How we handle the invoicing and money collection is an important process in the business and needs to be stress free and easy. Many of our clients have excessive levels of stress in their lives, including financial stresses. If the payment process is efficient and without hassle then it does not become a focal point for the client. Having EFTPOS and credit card facilities can enable this but does cost to run. With today's technology, most clients can automatically transfer funds on their phones or at minimum by computer at home. It is important, however, to get clients to identify their payments so you are aware of who has and has not paid. Having your banking details on a take home form is a great way to work with your clients and then they can actually pay before their sessions.

Having proper invoices and receipts available at the time of payment is crucial to keeping client confidence in your processes. Efficient invoicing is also an asset to your practice and maintaining up-to-date and concise records will save a great deal of time when it comes to completing taxation records.

I fully recommend using an electronic accounting package of some kind for ease of use. There are some great industry specific packages now that not only complete your invoices, but also work as appointment book, client records and accounting systems. While these packages may be costly to set up, the time you save using such a system makes them very cost effective.

All the designing of your processes for your business takes time and some of them evolve with time. In order to achieve everything required, it is essential, that this in itself be planned. It is very advisable to make a timeline with action points so this process becomes achievable. I found in setting up my own practice that many of these procedures needed to be in place before opening the doors. Some needed to be updated regularly and some could wait for those days when things were not so busy.

When I first began and time-lined all that needed to be achieved, I found that prioritising tasks was beneficial. I was then able to accomplish the important things first.

This does not mean that I always achieved all of the action points on my timeline. I distinctly remember the first time I had my notes subpoenaed. I had foreseen this event and had added to my action points the format that I would use for this scenario. I had even researched the requirements and had notes on how best to meet such a request. I simply had not had (or made) the time to complete this task. I felt I was flying by the seat of my pants addressing that first subpoena. This definitely affected my confidence. I made time very soon after this event to complete the action point and over time the pro-forma sheet for addressing subpoenas gave me much more confidence. I felt prepared.

This list tends to be never-ending. Even when I sold my practice there were things on the priority list that needed attending to, forms that needed updating, a business plan review, research into pricing of insurances etc. This timeline became my to-do list and was very helpful in maintaining my practice.

CHAPTER 14
THE BEST PLAN-PROFITABILITY

Although it's usually the last part of your business plan, the financial strategy is often the most important factor in determining the viability of your practice and if you have enough resources to seed your practice or whether you'll be able to secure any funding or investment. Let's face it, if your practice is not going to make you money then it isn't a long-term possibility and there will be expenses before your practice makes any money.

Decisions need to be made and budgets formulated and put in place to achieve your practice's objectives. These include information in relation to the financial resources required to set up and open your practice. A comprehensive analysis of costs required to set up an office, meet all operating requirements, like insurance and original costs such as printing and the marketing required to attract your first clients takes time and thought.

The capital investments such as office furniture are obvious expenses. Some consideration should be given to advertising signage, enabling clients to find you. There are also considerations like telephone lines, internet connections and EFTPOS connections. It is important to be seen as professional from your first client, so your accounting/booking/calendar system is another setup expense. Then you have rent or, for the very fortunate, the purchase of an office. Both of these options have associated costs, which need to be budgeted for. It is imperative that you are aware of the total costs involved. Many leased properties also have outgoings to be covered, like water and taxes. Being very clear about these extras can save a lot of heartache.

This list of expenses can become a very long list and, once again, prioritising may be necessary. Start with the essentials and build from there. It can actually be a while until your practice is making a living for you, unless your pay is a priority. Mostly, money made needs to be reinvested in the practice until it has been fully developed.

The secret to success is actually knowing this and being aware of when your practice will be making those returns. Setting financially realistic objectives, forecasting profit and loss figures, understanding your practice's financial position (balance sheet) and having a handle on cash flow and breakeven analysis are all a part of planning your practice.

There is a real danger in entering into a practice, when you want to succeed and build, if you do not understand the taxation implications. I am aware of one small practice who did not think they should be charging GST on their services. As the business grew, and dutifully did their annual tax return, the powers that be were alerted to the fact that proper paperwork and – therefore proper accounts – had not been kept. While the GST collected and the GST paid were similar amounts, and only a few hundred dollars were outstanding, the fine for not complying was an added expense, and obviously not budgeted for. This could have been the end of this practice had the proper advice from an expert allowing a payment plan not been attained.

Many of us are not great planners when it comes to financial matters. Most of us really do not desire to be the expert when it comes to bookkeeping. If this is you, outsource this task. Sure, learn from your expert, but unless you have a solid background in accounting, leave it to an expert.

❧❦

As stated earlier, the last stage of the planning process is the summary page, which actually appears near the front of your plan for outsiders who view your plan. Now you have done all your research, made all the important decisions and chosen the path for your practice, this becomes an easy exercise.

The use of such a business plan when setting up a counselling practice is a time and energy consumer. It is also a time, energy and stress saver in the long term. It gives you parameters to work within and timelines with which to operate your practice. There is no doubt in my mind that my practice would not have succeeded without its plan and I feel the plan was a great success as I now look back at setting up, operating and selling the practice. It enabled me to work within guidelines, which gave me confidence and answers when things were not all sunshine and roses. It kept the practice on an even keel, even in rough seas.

Semper minatur
Forever planning

SECTION 3

EMBRACING

CHAPTER 15
ETHICAL PRACTICE

My practice, though planned thoroughly, still delivered dilemmas. I guess, even with all the forethought, I was naïve when working with clients. The units I studied relating to ethics and codes of conduct did not prepare me for the real world of counselling. The challenges of counselling had me doing more research and self-discovery.

It was very easy, when studying, to agree with a statement without testing yourself. Similarly, when reading a code of conduct it is easy to read the words and not question exactly what they mean in the real world, especially when you have not experienced that real world yet. I am going to quote the Australian Counselling Association's Code of Ethics and Practice because it is the one I used. An example of this is the first requirement in the code of ethics to

> *"Offer a non-judgemental professional service, free from discrimination, honouring the individuality of the client."*

On first reading, and even after revisiting my study notes and extra reading on ethics, my immediate reaction to this requirement is, "Sure, no problems. I can do that." However, on closer inspection, in the real world, I was not as confident.

Non-judgemental—what does that really mean? According to the Webster Dictionary, it means, "avoiding judgements based on one's personal and especially moral standards." Now, the fact that we base these judgements on personal standards surely invites subjective judgement.

When I was in high school, I participated in our annual sports carnival every year. When I was in year eight, I donned my green faction shirt, ready to compete; I arrived at the school bus stop. There were three fellow students waiting to catch the bus, all wearing their red faction shirts. These shirts were that yellow-based red that washes out eventually to look orange. That morning, the red shirts bullied me mercilessly. I arrived at school bruised and battered and in no fit condition to compete, confidence completely shattered. To this day, when I see that yellow-based red, the fear balls in the pit of my stomach.

If a client were to walk through my door wearing that yellow-based red, would I be completely capable of non-judgement? Would I be totally honouring the individuality of the client? Can I practice free from discrimination with that ball in the pit of my stomach?

I thought many times about the thoughts that may prevent me from honestly adhering to this ethical requirement. I have worked on these thoughts to the point where I can say, "Yes, I can offer these things to my client." That ball in my stomach belongs to an event decades ago, and is very irrelevant to any client who walks through the door, but I definitely needed to explore this and be sure in my own mind that this was the case.

We all have past experiences, both good and not so good. Therefore, we have preconceived responses to particular occurrences in our lives. This can cause us to be judgemental, to discriminate and to affect our receptiveness of another person. We are human. I think our responsibility here is to be self-aware, to know our limitations and our strengths and to minimize the effects of our past on our clients.

First impressions come from these preconceived responses. We all make those snap second decisions about people and situations; it is human nature. In our professional capacity though, we have to be aware of this process and act accordingly.

I distinctly remember pulling myself up for being judgemental and discriminatory. This situation reflected my personal situation. At the time, my son was going through the trend of wearing his jeans so his underwear showed. We had a conversation about the trend and agreed that some minimal showing of the waistband was acceptable. This was definitely a compromise. I really did not like this fashion trend at all but my son was embracing the style. When a new client came to my office with his jeans well down his thighs, the conversation with my son echoed in my head. I will be the first to admit that, in the conversation with my son, I spoke with judgement and questioned social acceptability; we discussed family values. I did not have the same right to question this person's fashion sense and the stereotype this could lead me to conceive. This did not prevent the thoughts, so fresh from my chat with my son, from entering my head. I simply had to recognise the difference between the two situations.

Another situation where I am certain I can say prejudice was not an issue, but apprehension was present, was with a sixteen-year-old boy who came into my office. This boy was very in control and made a point of ensuring the things we discussed were confidential. I went over the rules of confidentiality twice and he seemed happy to continue. He also made a point of letting me know that he was paying for counselling himself and his family were unaware that he was there.

Once the boundaries were set to both of our satisfaction, the boy relaxed into the armchair and began talking. He was very matter of fact. He shared that he believed in Islam and that his parents disagreed with some of the teachings he was following. Warning signals flashed! All the television infomercials came to me in an instant, "Be alert, not alarmed." Once we started to explore the teachings he spoke of, I realised this boy was like any other teenager, trying to define his own set of values. His confusion was about honesty. He felt his parents, who were deeply religious, were not always honest with him. This was confusing him and we looked at the passages from the Koran that he was quoting. This intelligent young man and I then entered into a long discussion on how literally we take religion.

We both learned a lot that day and, when I reflected after the session, I decided that, yes, I had judged. We all have fears. Was I prejudiced against this boy and his religion? No, I was aware of radicalism and my fear had been for this possibility. It had nothing to do with this boy being Islamic. This young man attended three more sessions, each looking for clarity on how his beliefs influenced his values.

This inward looking dissection of our thinking makes non-judgement possible. We can think with biases sometimes and yet act without discrimination in our professional life. We can honour the individuality of each client only if we continually challenge our thoughts.

Another concept I have questioned continually is that of offering advice. The second requirement of the code of ethics is to

> *"Establish the helping relationship in order to maintain the integrity and empowerment of the client without offering advice."*

I fully understand that we cannot ethically do the "if I were you, I would…" or the "the best thing for you is…" I have also been careful to avoid the extremes like must, always and should. These are generally the indicators of advice, and undermine the clients' integrity, but I have often questioned the provision of strategies as the offering of advice.

Let me see if I can explain my confusion here. Take the example of a client who comes to talk about their issues with coping in their life. They talk about stresses, challenges and the effect these have on their lives. This may be things like interrupted sleep, isolation or mood swings. They have obviously come to see us to off load about their issues but also to resolve them. In a situation like this, I would possibly ask, "Which one of these symptoms causes the biggest issue?" For the example's sake, if the client suggests that they would cope better from a good night's sleep, we would address this. Sure, we would see if they have the ability to solve it themselves; we might ask them what has worked in the past; we might even enquire what things have changed to get the client thinking and solving for himself or herself; we would empower them.

However, if the client were unable to solve the issue on their own, we would offer strategies to assist. Yes, we would give a range of strategies allowing the client to decide their own remedy, but we would still be offering up a set of knowledge from which they will choose. We would be asking them to try one of our alternatives. Are these not alternatives of our advice?

Each may be well-researched options, and they may differ from those given by another counsellor. We give these options hoping the client will recognise a solution for him or herself. Does this not make them advice? Is this not our solution to their problem? I guess my question here is how is suggesting a client tries a sensory meditation for sleep or listens to calming music not advice and just a suggestion?

The answer I found worked for me was in the saying. If I were to say, "I think you should try a meditation," then this felt like advice. However, if I were to say, "I know of a great meditation that may help," and wait for the client to ask for more information, then this is only suggestion. This may seem like semantics to some; however, if we take our code of ethics seriously then consideration of these definitions becomes important. Many times, I simply gave the client information sheets on sleeping and allowed them to do the reading of the options and decide for themselves.

I think the avoidance of giving advice is about the choices. If we make choices for our client then we are giving advice; if we give options and allow the client the choice then we are making suggestions.

If I am truly honest, however, there were times when I felt advice was appropriate. A client comes to mind who came to me for some parenting issues. Her 6-year-old son came with her. The mother began the session by stating that the stepfather, her new partner, hated the boy and wanted her to send him away to live either with his father or to boarding school. I did advise her that this was a conversation best had without her son in the room as his hurt was very visible, but she insisted on continuing. Watching the effect this was having on her son made me very uncomfortable, and, eventually, I escorted him to another room to colour in. Returning to the room, I explained that counsellors had a responsibility to do no harm and that continuing the session as she requested was harming her son. I suggested some different formats, counselling for herself, couples counselling and even family counselling. I allowed her to decide, but I had still given her advice. I had made the choice for her.

Many clients enter the consultation room asking for advice. While the session does belong to the client and it is important to know exactly what a client expects from a session, it is up to the counsellor to set the boundary when it comes to offering advice. A conversation with a client regarding the expectations they hold can also include the limits under which counsellors work. I have had clients who continually request advice. One client I worked with persistently asked for advice. After having the conversation about not wanting to advise her, I explained that we could look at her options and we began listing them on the whiteboard. This became a bit of a joke in our sessions and whenever she asked, "What do you think?" or, "What is your advice?" we would move immediately to the whiteboard. This client took this strategy home with her as a method of making tough decisions.

Another issue I have found with advice is in my role as supervisor of other counsellors. Many times, I have counsellors ask for my advice on issues they face with clients. What counsellors have to recognise is that supervisors have not been sitting in the room with these clients. While supervisors have experience and training, they do not know the clients of their supervisees. Again, I offer options in these cases. The first option is answering your own question. Explore options yourself; I can guide you in this but you need to explore yourself so you are empowered for future clients, forever learning. If a counsellor is truly stuck, as can happen from time to time, then I can help by giving some options too. It would be negligent of me, however, to give advice on a client, especially one I have never met.

❧

One area that has caused me to revise boundaries, and in which I have found little direction, is the issue of counselling at arm's length. There is no definition when it comes to this issue in the code of ethics. In fact, it does not get a mention. This is a presumed boundary and over the years, this has needed clarification for me. I now have a very clear picture of arm's length and I have very long arms.

The first time arm's length became an issue for me was very early on in my practice. I had worked with the son of a friend in an assignment when I was studying parenting and family counselling. As I was not yet a counsellor, and our tutor advised us to work with a child we knew, I had no issue with this. I worked with this family on an up-and-go program to get to school on time in the mornings. The assignment went very well and the family were extremely happy to have this issue solved and for free! The real issue was when, two years later, the family were once again having issues with their son and they wanted to come and see me professionally.

Now, I was a practicing professional with a code of ethics to follow, and, with my own boundaries of arm's length, I felt this was inappropriate. I spoke with the family and explained the concept of arm's length and the fact that it was to protect both them and me. They understood and were happy to accept a referral to a colleague.

Arm's length also became an issue for me when I accepted a new client, a newly married couple, whose names I did not recognise. On their arrival at the first session, I recognised the woman as the ex-wife of one of my husband's employees. I had some knowledge of the bitter break up from her ex-husband and did not feel comfortable with the situation. Although I had only met this woman once, very briefly, it felt like the relationship was too close to home. I referred this couple also.

Many counsellors who I supervise, particularly those just setting up their practices, have issues with arm's length. There is quite a common approach to start a practice by word of mouth, friends of friends. This seemed to me not to honour the idea of arm's length. If we cannot counsel family and friends, just how far does this extend?

A case that comes to mind here involves a counsellor who chose to counsel a friend's sister. This then extended to this woman's whole family. As the counselling sessions progressed, the counsellor found evidence of a sexual abuse incident with the nine-year-old daughter. As was required, the counsellor mandatorily reported the incident, which involved a nephew living in the same house. This, of course, rocked this whole extended family and the counsellor's friend became involved. There was no arm's length relationship in this case now, if it ever existed.

When this counsellor came to supervision and disclosed the situation, it was too late to make a call on whether this was arm's length or not. I suggested to her to immediately refer this case, disclose the arm's length situation to the Department of Chid Protection, who were now involved, and cut communication with the friend. This action caused the family more confusion and angst. This counsellor may have avoided the situation had she been aware of the implications of the boundary she had set.

Do not get me wrong here. It is not my job to judge whether this action was ethical or not. My job is simply to help the counsellor in this situation, firstly to solve the presented dilemma, and secondly guide them to look at the boundaries they have set for themselves. These boundaries are different for each counsellor. I challenge my supervisees to look at these boundaries and ensure both they and their clients are protected and safe.

Related to arm's length is the concept of dual roles. Is it OK to counsel the man who services my car? What about having someone as a client who volunteers at the same not-for-profit I volunteer at on weekends? Is it ethical to counsel the man who runs the corner shop? Many people have roles in our lives that do not prevent them from being our clients. For me, it is about the relationship I have with these people. If the man who services my car, not sure of his name but I have seen him at the workshop, walks through my practice door, then I do not have an issue seeing him. However, if James, who services my car at home and with whom I enjoy a coffee when he finishes his work, walks through the door, then, no, I will not see him as a client.

My hairdresser, with whom I have a great relationship, and with whom I chat non-stop when I am her client, asked for an appointment to work on relationship issues with her husband. I explained my boundary of arm's length and dual roles and referred her to a colleague. Friendly gossip in the salon chair and counselling do not belong in the same relationship. For me, these boundaries are very clear and static. They do not move. However, I have spoken to many counsellors who are not sure of these boundaries and take a case-by-case approach. I could not do this as it would emotionally weaken my decisions without the boundaries in place and feel I would make exceptions that may cross the ethical line. I guess I feel more secure knowing my boundaries.

CHAPTER 16
SECURITY

Speaking of feeling secure, this is another area where many counsellors seem unprepared. Personal security in your practice is an important issue. Whether you are working alone or others are in the office, feeling safe is a basic right. It is your responsibility to put measures in place to ensure both your safety and the feeling of safety. In my practice, which was in an industrial estate, safety was never really an issue for me. I had an alarm on the premises, which also doubled as a panic alarm. Fortunately, I never needed to use this alarm but did set it off by mistake one day. It was great to realise that help was less than five minutes away. This was very reassuring and made me feel safe.

I also had a couple of less technological measures in place. In the adjoining office, five men ran a wine and spirit warehouse. I met these men very soon after setting up my practice. One of the men suggested to me that, if ever I was in trouble, I could just bang on the wall and they would come running to my rescue … very gallant.

I never needed this service either, but knew they were serious. One day, I decided to put some new art on the office wall. My banging in of the nail caused three men to come running into my office. Once again, I had my sense of security boosted.

The other security measure, of which I was very ignorant for two years, was the eyes on the street. Across the road from my practice was a newspaper printer. There was a manned security gate, which operated twenty-four-seven. The night watchman, who I usually waved to as I was leaving work, came over for a chat one night when I stayed after my last client to write up a report. He had been concerned because my behaviour had not followed its normal pattern; I usually would leave within half an hour of my last client. We sat and shared a cup of coffee as he explained to me that the security guards had been concerned for me, a woman alone at night with clients. They had been looking out for me from the day I started my practice! I agreed that, from then on, if I was going to stay back to do reports I would just come out, give them a wave, and let them know so they knew I was all right. More knights in shining armour!

I had always let my family know when I would be home and would ring as I was leaving work to let them know I was on my way home. I know this is a safety measure but felt I was doing this more for their peace of mind than for my safety. I was also very aware in the office of my safety, particularly in an initial session when I did not yet know the client. I would always have an escape route from my office. This was not difficult as my office had two doors and I could easily escape if necessary.

I have to say this sense of safety was challenged a couple of times. The first time I felt unsafe, however, I was probably more concerned for my client. My client, a woman in her 40s, was in for her third session. She had presented with confusion over where her life was headed, particularly in her work, and how this was affecting her family. There was nothing to suggest trouble in her relationship; in fact, she had said this part of her life was the motivation for her to change other areas. As we sat talking, the front door of the practice opened and the bell tinkled. We continued talking, blissfully unaware that her husband was in reception. Suddenly, my office door flew open. The tallest, stockiest, red-faced man stood in the doorway. I instinctively stood between him and my client. He started yelling. My client started crying.

My training in difficult situations reminded me to stay calm. I remained between the two and began the "talk to the emotions" protocol I had learned.

"You look really angry."

"You bet I'm f***ing angry!" he yelled back at me.

"I can see something has upset you." I was trying to show a calmness I did not feel.

"Yeh, she is going to leave me, isn't she?"

"I think you are feeling a bit confused about why your wife is seeing a counsellor." I could see him calming down now.

"Would you like to join us for a chat? Is that OK?" (I asked my client for her permission.) We all sat down and clarified the position for this husband scared of losing his wife. In later sessions, I was able to laugh at this situation with my clients but, at the time, it did challenge my security.

The only other time I felt afraid at the practice was a time that made me look at my prejudices. I had taken a call from a man who was quite distraught. He had just found out he was a father to a seven-year-old boy. The boy's mother had recently passed away and her family had notified the authorities of his connection. The family did not want anything to do with this child, who according to them was a wild animal, neglected by his drug-addicted mother. The man initially wanted counselling for the boy, who had not stopped crying since he had met his father, and then some help with how to parent.

I suggested he brought his son in and we would assess the situation. We booked a session for two o'clock that afternoon. As I prepared for this session, there was a loud rumble outside, not unusual in the industrial estate, but very loud indeed. I looked out the front door to see about forty bikies in our car park. My heart raced. The other counsellor was concerned. She disappeared out to the kitchen. If I am honest, I was frightened. I looked at the panic button on the alarm for reassurance.

A man came through the door with a young boy in tow. The boy was tiny and looked about four years old. He hid behind the man's leg. The man was dressed in leathers with patches. He was obviously a member of a bikie gang.

The words that came from this man and the tenderness in his voice caught me by surprise. He was extremely concerned about the welfare of his newly discovered son. It all seemed quite incongruent with his appearance. As we spoke, he turned around and waved at his friends outside and the rumble echoed around the office as the bikies drove off. The man just said, "They are concerned and wanted to make sure we were alright." We went into the office and began the session. Over time, I came to realise that this child had gained a completely new extended family who cared about him and his wellbeing.

I had to look at the feelings I experienced that day, and see the prejudice in my fear. I learnt, over time, that this man was a generous, caring father. I had only seen the bikie. During the many sessions I had with this boy, and the sessions I had with other children of these bikies, I learnt that this community really cherished their children. When I see a bikie now, I have a more tolerant viewpoint and am not so quick to judge. They are the proverbial village.

I was, however, more secure in that moment of fear because of the security precautions I had put in place. I often wonder how this scenario would unfold if I had a practice set up in my living room at home. I also wonder what security precautions home practitioners have in place for times like these. They do not have three guys next door who would come running; they do not have a security guard across the street keeping an eye on them; I am not even sure they would have a panic button in easy access. How do they know their next client is not someone who may challenge their sense of security?

❧

I just want to back track a little at this point to the arm's length case I mentioned where there was a mandatory report. This is another area where I find many counsellors ill prepared. We all know the circumstances when we need to mandatory report; however, unless we have had to do this, most counsellors know little of the process. Many work on the need-to-know logic but I question the wisdom of this. In that moment when you are with a client who reveals such an incident, I would think knowing exactly what the procedure is, with phone numbers on hand, would help to lessen the trauma both for the client and for the counsellor.

I have only had to use this procedure a couple of times but felt confident in doing so. It is not an easy thing to do and red tape questions can dint confidence along the way. This is why it is a great idea to enter into the process confident from the start. We are affecting people's lives in a big way when we undertake this responsibility and should not take it lightly. I know of a situation where a practitioner googled the process in front of the client. This does not instil confidence in the counsellor for the client and I should imagine it was quite uncomfortable for all involved.

Counsellors should familiarise themselves with such important processes. Similarly, the panic I hear from counsellors the first time their notes are subpoenaed is preventable. Preparation for such events is simply a couple of hours of research. We have a responsibility to know how to comply with the requirements of our system.

Additionally, we have a responsibility to know how the legal system works and how this may affect our clients. Anyone who works with relationships and families should understand how the family law system works. I am not saying here that we need to study the law. I am simply saying we need to know how it works in regard to the clients we see. There are some good courses around on family law and counselling; if this is your area of expertise then learn the appropriate terminology and consequences for your client. If your client is proceeding through the family court, it is important you understand the processes of family dispute resolution, mediation and conciliation. If a client discusses a court order or parenting plan, your understanding of the process will help you understand their situation.

Similarly, understanding the difference between the various restraining orders and knowing exactly what they mean is useful information when dealing with traumatised people. Apprehended violence orders and a violence restraining orders have different outcomes for our clients and understanding how these affect our clients, without putting them through a description of the restrictions, is beneficial for our clients.

I had a situation arise once where a client had been court ordered to have counselling for an issue that had seen him arrested. As he had been a client of mine in the past, he had advised the court that he would like me to provide this counselling. Not a problem; we began our sessions and, in my naivety, I did not ask for any paperwork. This was because I was unaware that the court would ask for this paperwork to be completed. We worked through several sessions and, at the conclusion of one session, the client asked if he could continue with me, even though he had completed the court's required number of sessions. This rang an alarm bell for me. How was the court to know if the client met this condition? I asked the client whether there was any paperwork to fill in and he said he had a pile of paperwork, which he had not looked at.

Apparently, I was supposed to be giving weekly reports on the progress of this client and, after eight sessions, write a report for the court on the client's progress and my recommendations. I asked the client to contact the court to find out the best path for us to follow, since we had not met the conditions of his order. An officer of the court contacted me and I submitted the required paperwork, albeit late. I had learnt to check for paperwork for court ordered clients. I also became aware of the consequences of not filling in this paperwork, or filling it in incorrectly.

I had a court ordered client attend one of our parenting courses. This was a common occurrence as the family court recognised the course as a good parenting course. I ran the course over three consecutive Tuesday nights and the client did not attend the third session; however, she did phone to try to obtain her certificate of completion. I refused to issue the certificate, as she had not completed the course. The next day, I once again received a call from an officer of the court to inquire about my client. She had said she had attended the course but I was refusing to issue the certificate. When I explained the situation, the officer thanked me and explained that to issue the certificate falsely was actually contempt of court. I was glad I had insisted on the client completing the course to gain her certificate.

As you can see, it is vital to understand the legal requirements of our work. We do not have to know and understand all the laws, almost impossible, but to serve our clients well we need some knowledge.

Another interaction I had with the police was to ask for a welfare check on a client I was concerned about with respect to safety. The client was in a domestic violence situation and had been for four visits. She was in the process of leaving the situation and we had arranged a safe house. The client decided to stay one last weekend and was to come in for a session on the Monday. I had tried to convince her not to stay but it was her birthday and she hoped for some sort of miracle. When the client did not arrive for her appointment on the Monday, I called her mobile. When I got no answer, I sent her an email asking her to call me. I was quite concerned. When I had not heard from her by Tuesday morning, and she still was not answering her phone, I felt I should take action. I rang the local police and requested a welfare check. Originally, the police officer suggested that, if I had the address, I should pay a visit myself. I was not comfortable with doing this and when I explained this, the officer said yes, they would do a check. I was very relieved to hear that the home had lost power, phones were flat and no internet was working, but the client would contact me when she could. I questioned whether I had wasted police resources but the officer assured me that I had not and that they had laid some unrelated charges. I never heard back from this client.

My work with teenagers saw me at the local police station a couple of times, when teens I had been working with had requested my presence because their parents were unavailable. I developed a good working relationship with the local police station and I know this prevented a couple of teens from getting into real trouble. Funnily enough, I bumped into one of these teens, now in his mid-twenties, not so long ago. He is now a police officer!

CHAPTER 17
PROFESSIONAL PRACTICES

I have often reflected on what makes a practice professional and have decided that it is a combination of many small things. The way we dress and present to our clients is a personal choice but I feel it has an impact. Imagine going into a lawyer's office and seeing a lawyer dressed in jeans and a T-shirt. Generally, this would ring alarm bells, unless the lawyer worked casually in low socio-economic areas as some do. Some counsellors mistakenly believe that dressing casually puts clients at ease. While this may be true sometimes, we want others to treat us as professionals; we need to dress as professionals. I have actually had a counsellor tell me they dress more professionally to attend an Association meeting than when seeing clients. I understand the logic, to be professional with our peers, but why do we treat our time with clients differently?

Another issue that has me shaking my head when dealing with other counsellors is hand shaking. I often ran a workshop for teenage boys on socialisation and taught how to shake hands properly. Many struggle with this social and professional practice; no one teaches these niceties anymore and many do not get it right.

There are some basic rules to remember when shaking hands. Firstly, all handshakes require eye contact. This shows that the other person has your full attention. There is nothing more disconcerting when shaking hands than the other person looking elsewhere. Secondly, your handshake should be the same regardless of who you are shaking with, man, woman or child. It should be firm but not tight; your hand should remain vertical; two or three pumps is enough; the web between your thumb and forefinger should touch the other person's. Delicate little handshakes that only engage your fingers make the other person feel uncomfortable. Handshakes are more effective if you speak the person's name as you shake.

This may seem like a trivial matter, but a good handshake will establish good rapport with your client. Be the person who takes control of the handshake. The exception to this is obviously when shaking hands is culturally unacceptable and knowing when this is the case is important to master.

There also seems to be some confusion when it comes to contact with the client. Obviously, shaking hands is contact. This happens before we begin a session, the therapeutic relationship begins, and I believe it is acceptable. While working in a session, is it OK to make contact with the client? As a rule, I believe no. However, have I made contact with a client in a session, yes. One client, a seventy-year-old woman who was grieving the loss of her husband and the loss of her dog, and was sobbing uncontrollably, needed human contact. A hand on her shoulder as I passed her some more tissues was compassionate. We cannot be cold to our clients in times of need. However, an embrace or hug I feel is not appropriate. Similarly, a high five to a six-year-old who has worked hard in a session is building rapport and encouraging the change we were working at making. Again, a hug would be inappropriate. Working a lot with children, I have often been hugged by a child as they are leaving. When this type of contact is unavoidable, it is important to move so the hug is side on and you make minimal contact. I also make a rule of discussing this with the child in the next session and make an alternative available, like making a secret handshake or giving a high five.

I have a bowl of sweets in my office, which teenagers and many adults help themselves to. This is their decision and I know it helps many of them to talk more freely. However, I feel to have these freely available to child clients is also inappropriate. I move them on to a side cupboard when I have child clients. Naturally, some children sniff them out and ask for them. I always make this the parents' decision at the conclusion of the session. Requiring the child to ask the parent for permission often has mixed results. Many parents are completely fine with their child eating sweets but I also found some were against this for their children. Most appreciated being able to make the decision. Some children would bring in snacks to share in a session and I am OK with them eating while we work but did not partake myself. One young girl even baked me my own cupcake, which I accepted but did not eat in the session.

This brings me to the accepting of gifts as thanks for service. I have many cards and letters thanking me for my work with clients. I treasure them as these usually represent the difficult cases I have had in my practice. Clients have also given me gifts, thanking me for my work, and even parcels for Christmas. I have accepted handmade gifts from children, flowers and some homemade cookies. One client, who was a chef, even made me a cake to share with my family for Christmas, which I accepted. I graciously decline any other gifts.

I had a client who I had seen for almost two years and, when we decided no more sessions were necessary, I received a card in the mail. It had a lovely message inside and I was delighted with this. It also had a gift card for two hundred dollars. I could not accept this. I rang the client and explained that the accepting of gifts was unethical and I could not accept the gift card. We came to a compromise and took the gift card to a local charity to use. This was an acceptable way of the client showing appreciation and the charity was extremely grateful.

Christmas time is a time for giving and many clients are very generous. When I explain the situation, most clients are happy to donate their gift to charity and some years I dropped off a whole box of beautifully wrapped gifts to be distributed. I really appreciate the sentiment behind these gifts and encourage clients to write cards or letters because these I can accept and keep.

CHAPTER 18
ADEQUATE ACCESS

What is adequate access for your clients? Many of our clients are in need of many things; some demand more time and attention than others do. How available should we be? What are our rights and responsibilities? How do we set this boundary? Is this boundary flexible?

Some relatively easy strategies make this an easy boundary to set. The first of these is to separate your phone number; have one phone for work and another for your personal calls. You can easily turn the work phone off when you are not available for work. Many counsellors fear missing clients if we do not answer the phone, but if you have a good answering service or a professional message on your phone, clients will leave a message or contact you again. A professional message on the phone should include a greeting, office hours, reassurance that the client is important and emergency numbers. This gives the client the message that you are a compassionate counsellor who values clients.

The other problem with not turning work phones off is that, as a counsellor, you are then always available to clients. This may well be great for your clients and may gain new clients but giving up your downtime is also opening the door for compassion fatigue. We all need to be able to turn off and revitalise. Burnout is dangerous and this is not acting in the best interest of the client or yourself.

Setting firm office hours is also important, for both efficiency and self-care. I found many clients required after hours appointments and to accommodate this I opened the office until eight o'clock some evenings. This meant starting late some days as working from nine in the morning until eight at night was too long a day to be effective. Saturday morning sessions were also popular, so while I was in the practice alone, I always took Fridays off in lieu and worked Saturday mornings. Once I had another counsellor on board, of course, I could offer longer opening hours and we could work shifts. It was critical, though, that we both maintained our downtime and did not allow client demand to extend our working hours.

This became more complex when we had several Employee Assistance Programs (EAPs), which guaranteed the availability of a counsellor within twenty-four hours. We overcame this by leaving time in our calendars for emergencies. If there were no clients for this time, it simply became paperwork time or research time. We did not work outside our designated working hours often. One exception when we made this rule more flexible was in a dire emergency. This happened twice in the whole time I had the practice. The first time was when I was a sole operator and received a call to an industrial accident at the premises of one of my EAP clients. Ambulances took two injured workers to hospital but the young workforce at this site were all in shock. The employer rightly did not want to send them home until they had seen someone. Some of them definitely should not have been driving home in the state they were in after what they had witnessed. I spent the whole day on site until I had seen all the workers, singularly and in groups, and management had safely sent them home in taxis.

The management also wanted me to meet with the two men in hospital and their families. I was exhausted and was in two minds about whether to continue or to find help. Management rang the hospital who recommended counselling the following day, so, much to my relief, I went home, re-organised clients for the following day and went to bed. This situation had pushed me to a limit and I made plans to cope more effectively with this sort of situation in the future. It was a steep learning curve for me.

The other situation was with a pro-bono client. This was an animal welfare group who looked after native animals. Unfortunately, we suffered a dreadful bushfire season and the authorities called in this group of animal lovers to rescue burnt and homeless native animals. Much to the despair of this group, this mission turned into a mostly euthanasia exercise where most of the animals had to be put down and quickly. The authorities issued rifles and the group came home devastated with what they had witnessed and done. I got a call at seven o'clock in the evening, after a long day at the office. My employed counsellor was still at the office with clients. Using the emergency plan I had created after the industrial accident, I called in another counsellor and we both attended the animal welfare workers. Although I was exhausted by the time I went home, the emergency plan had more than halved the work for me and I was extremely grateful to the other counsellor for being available at such short notice.

Some counsellors I have spoken with have suggested that they would not work at their best in situations like these. My advice to them is simple; do not sign up to EAPs that may require emergency work. It is a choice.

I have had a couple of counsellors who work outside their normal office hours for clients in need, and even allow after hours phone calls to a private number. In a small practice with limited numbers of clients, this may be acceptable. Once again, this is a choice. I would only suggest that, once the boundaries are blurred, it becomes easier to blur them more next time. I think flexibility is a great master, but beware of becoming its slave.

CHAPTER 19
PROFESSIONAL NETWORKING

I have often wondered how some counsellors operate in their isolation. Several of the counsellors I supervises network in very limited circles. Many of them have never considered peer supervision as a networking tool, most of them attend very few professional development events and for some the monthly Association meetings is the only time they talk with other counsellors. This is such a shame because the counselling world is full of people who have incredible knowledge and experience. There seems to be a roadblock to sharing this information and a hesitation to engage with other professionals. I am fortunate to have an extremely vast network of counsellors and other mental health workers. I have consciously cultivated these relationships, which have increased my knowledge incredibly. I am in touch with people in England, the USA and Europe. I have a great network in Australia, mainly with people I have met at conferences or contacted when I have read their work. To grow continually, I think we need to make these connections and foster relationships with other professionals.

Over the years, these relationships have been rewarding for me. I recently referred a counsellor in Melbourne, who I met at a conference in Sydney, to a hypnotherapist I met when he spoke at a conference I attended in Brisbane—with great outcomes!

I guess one of my strongest networks is the counsellors I supervises. One of the advantages for me in supervising other counsellors is that I learn from them, and sometimes refer to them. These are all intelligent professionals who have knowledge and experience to share and I am fortunate to know them. I am also confident that my supervisees gain value from our relationship.

I am often disappointed when I hear some counsellors talk about professional development. For some counsellors this is just a mandatory condition of staying registered with their association. I wish they could see the opportunities this sort of education and networking afford us. We often encourage our clients to open their eyes and see the positive aspect, but many of us are not fantastic at doing this ourselves. I am always encouraged at Association meetings when a counsellor approaches another counsellor and asks for information or an opinion. These meetings are such a wonderful opportunity for expanding our knowledge, and they are free. Professional development is a state of mind, not an attendance at a function.

Recently, at our Association meeting, we had a very interesting speaker who shared lots of knowledge. Many counsellors spent the session writing notes and soaking up the information. I had a whole bag full of questions about the topic involved and was disappointed when question time came that no one else had questions. They seemed to have their quota of information and wanted no more. I felt this was a lost opportunity for so many of these counsellors.

I emailed the speaker with my questions and we continue to correspond. I hoped others would also stay in touch with this speaker but it seems none has. This makes me question their motivation for professional development.

These same counsellors, I find, are not very good at sharing their knowledge either. They protect what works for them like trade secrets. One of the best networking activities I have been involved in was an activity called Tool Shed. We organised a group of counsellors to meet every second month with the express goal of sharing information, strategies and techniques. This was a fantastic group and every meeting four people would present their favourite tools. I learnt many different strategies and ideas and gained information about modalities, which I later developed more. Not only was this an opportunity to learn, it was inspiration to learn even more. This was a place to learn and practice new techniques, run by the group, was free and was probably the most interesting professional development I attended. A couple of students joined this group and their feedback was extremely positive, saying practical information like this was difficult to find.

Another interesting networking exercise I was involved in was through my local council. The child health nurse asked me to give a short chat to new mothers about how to recognise postnatal depression. The day I presented this talk, many other speakers were present. There was a child psychologist discussing ages and stages, a speech pathologist, an occupational therapist, a paediatric chiropractor and several nurses speaking on a range of subjects from sleep to diet to massage. I stayed the whole day and learned a lot. As a group of professionals, we decided to form a Facebook group and share our work. We corresponded often, frequently debating and solving issues as a group. We also referred to each other as was needed. Once a year, we all get together socially and have supported each other for over five years. This is one of my favourite networks and I will continue correspondence even into retirement. I guess the message here is not to limit your network to counselling professionals.

I have several networks that have evolved over time. The first was an alliance with my local high school, which is where my first clients came from. The pastoral care unit at this school are very pro-active and they have approached me to help with several issues. Some of these I provided free, like helping year 11 students set up a display for mental health week. Others I charged for, like speaking to the children about cyber bullying and sexting. The school were happy to help me with a project the on Act, Belong, Commit Program. This relationship has been mutually beneficial and I am aware that the school recommends me to its parents.

Another network that has benefitted me enormously is a group of mental health workers who all attended a small workshop at a conference years ago. We just seemed to click and decided to stay in touch. It is such a diverse group, a police chaplain, a drug rehabilitator, a school psychologist, a social worker in the navy, a weight loss hypnotherapist, a child expert for the family court and me. We regularly conference call; we are not all always available, but we do stay in touch via emails as well. This group are such good storytellers and share their knowledge generously and I feel privileged to belong to this group.

I once sat down and reviewed my networks, listing all the people I counted as belonging to one of my networks. I was pleased with the very long list I developed. I then took a critical look at the list. I looked at what I had given to each person and what I had received from each person in my networks. This was a time consuming exercise and, to begin with, I was unsure why I was actually doing it. When I had finished, however, there were some obvious holes in my network. One that struck me and made me re-evaluate was the lack of people in my network who had knowledge of adolescents, which was one of my specialties. Although this still is the case, I am an avid reader of all things teen and adolescent. In a world where things are changing second by second, adolescents are the pioneers of a completely new world and sufferers of the inherent issues that new technology brings. These new world problems are difficult to keep up with, but they are real and teens and adolescents are bringing them to counselling sessions. As I write this, my mind is screaming, *Network more in this!*

I also looked at the people on this list who I felt had not been as giving in our relationship. At the end of the process, I decided they were in the network for a reason; we do not all give equally; it is OK that some people were in my network as receivers. Maybe they passed things on within their own network. There were also people in the network I was uncertain had received much from being in my network. I decided they too were there for reasons of their own and that is all right.

CHAPTER 20

COMPLICATIONS OF EXPANSION

As we have already seen, part of my plan was to expand my practice and have other counsellors work in my practice. This goal caused me much angst that actually kept me awake at nights. With this goal, I was affecting someone else's professional life. I took this very seriously. I had a couple of occasions when I had had contracted counsellors because I had too much work for one person. This had worked out well and I had enjoyed the company at the practice. The decision to share work was difficult. How do you select someone to whom you can entrust your clients? How do you trust them with the reputation that you have worked so hard to establish? I felt it could all be lost in the blink of an eye. This was a time when networking proved invaluable. The couple of counsellors I contracted during busy times were both people I had met through networking. The first was a counsellor I had studied with and had developed a relationship with once we graduated. The second was actually a supervisor I had done some sessions with and who I knew was looking for extra work. Because I knew both these counsellors quite well I felt the risk diminish.

These counsellors both worked well in my practice and neither become entwined in the management of the business. They were purely counselling. This fitted the purpose perfectly. There were several occasions as my business grew when these counsellors worked with me. Neither, however, were suitable for full-time work in the practice.

As the business grew, and my work diversified, however, the need for extra personnel was obvious. I was at risk of overworking, burnout and I was struggling to fit all the clients into my working hours. I was concerned that I might not be able to meet my obligations of service within twenty-four hours for some of my EAPs. The need for a full-time counsellor became urgent.

I made the decision to subcontract a counsellor rather than employ, mainly to save on paperwork, for taxation implications and to save on the expenses that come with employment like worker's compensation and insurance. I had thoroughly researched the options when I did my business plan and, with the help of my accountant, made the decision to subcontract.

The next issue was complex. *How do I decide whom to have working in my practice?* I set up extensive criteria. I revised this list repeatedly before I was finally happy with the requirements for a contractor. I met a woman who I had instant rapport with and, after meeting a couple of times, decided that she met all the criteria I had set. I approached her with the idea of starting in the practice part time and building up over time as things developed.

Before this contractor began work, I needed to put some more thought into the ethics and procedures of a practice that supported more than one person. How was I to decide who saw which clients? What ratio of client contact time, administration and research would work for both of us? How involved in the administration of the practice was I encouraging this contractor to be? How should this evolve? What new procedures did I need to implement now I was not flying solo? How did sharing office space affect ethics, like confidentiality? How would the procedures in the day-to-day running of the office change with the introduction of another person? I needed to take some time to consider all the questions that arose from this decision. Sure, I had answers to some of them from when I had subcontracted earlier, but this was a more permanent situation and I felt it was quite different.

I focused primarily on the ethical dilemmas that sharing an office might cause. I was very aware that some confidentiality issues would arise. I had several high profile clients whose confidentiality had been a priority when first starting with me. The fact that I was a solo operator with no receptionist had been comforting for these clients and had enabled them to continue therapy. How would they feel with someone else in the office? How could I protect them from sharing a waiting room with other clients? Their wellbeing was the priority here and I found myself discussing this in session with the clients involved. We agreed that their sessions would be on days when the contractor was not in the office to begin with. I assured these clients that any counsellor who worked in the office understood fully the rules of confidentiality and that, once the contractor was full time, there should be no issue. All but one of the clients were satisfied with my explanation. This client felt uncomfortable with the chance that other clients might see them and I agreed to work after hours with this client. His concerns were real and I felt would affect his progress.

This client also brought up concerns about the confidentiality of his personal details and his file. This was something I had on my list to consider. When I was alone in the office, I could have files on my desk while I was writing up notes and doing administration work. This would have to change if I had another person in the office. I was also very aware that I needed to set up a separate filing system for the files of the contractor. Her promise to the client that their files were confidential was also important.

I had set up a system of sealed files for clients who had seen subcontracting counsellors in the past. I had also set up paperwork so that if a client returned to the practice after the subcontractor had left, I could gain written permission to open their file to facilitate further counselling. I used this same system with the new contractor. Over time, this system worked well and enabled clients to give permission so they could continue counselling with their new counsellor already having background knowledge of their case.

I did have a discussion at one stage with a subcontractor about who actually owned the client files. This counsellor was primarily concerned with the rights of her client. The client was actually a client of my practice and this counsellor was the attending counsellor. She had a very valid concern about the safety of the client notes, but they actually belonged in the practice. I implemented extra security, and this is why I sealed the files. I could only promise that ethically I would honour her promise to her client and, as a registered counsellor, I felt bound by the rules of confidentiality for all the clients who visited my practice. Her response was that she trusted my professionalism and was therefore satisfied with the measures I had in place. Her other option of taking the client files home with her was not secure and was riddled with problems.

An issue that challenged me ethically when I had a contractor working in the office was how I should decide which clients each of us saw. I specialised in children and teenagers, but was it fair that the contractor did not see any child or teen clients? This new contractor had experience in eating disorders, so did I give all these cases to her? I was aware that these decisions might limit growth and professional development. I recognised a need for balance, even in our specialised areas. I discussed this with the counsellor and she agreed that, while we should honour our specialties, we should not limit ourselves. We had the added ability to refer to each other if need be. This agreement also enabled us to teach each other in the areas we specialised in and share information.

I was also very protective of my EAP clients. Some of these contracts were difficult to attain and I was hesitant to risk them. To begin with, I was seeing all EAP clients. One of the benefits of having two counsellors working in the practice had to be that the office hours could be longer, but we did not both need to be in all the time. I could keep my Fridays off and still be covered at the office. This advantage also enabled me to let go of the exclusivity of the EAP work. When, on a Friday, an emergency call came for counselling from one of our EAP clients, I felt I had to stick to the boundaries I had set myself regarding days off. This meant that the other counsellor could see EAP clients. It was a leap of faith in her and after that first instance; this was never a concern again.

As our communication evolved, I recognised the need for an avenue for contractors to make suggestions and air complaints. I felt the need to give the contractor a voice if they felt I was being unfair or if they felt they knew a better way. We discussed this and decided to implement a performance review that we both undertook. This was both a good place for us both to recognise the other's strengths but also to discover the improvements we could both make. It was also a lot of fun as we usually discussed the results over lunch.

I was also concerned about the balance of power that inevitably occurs when there is more than one person in the workplace. After counselling in several workplaces, I was aware that personalities could have a huge effect on the workplace. I wanted a fair workplace where everyone had his or her voice heard, regardless of who owned the practice. Realistically, I knew many decisions were mine but, as I intended to train this counsellor to take over the practice, I also knew that I needed to share. I felt the most effective way to achieve this was to establish open communication about the practice. This was very effective and enabled the practice to expand as the contractor gained knowledge of the practice.

I also found that, in teaching someone else the mechanics of the practice, I had an opportunity to review some of the procedures and practices. Out came the business plan and reviews were made, amendments put in place. This really gave me a measure of how my practice was changing and growing.

This first contractor in my business also brought with her some new concepts for my practice. While I had always been aware of the environmental footprint of my business, this contractor was passionate about the environment. We made several changes to the running of the practice that improved our footprint and saved us money. The influence of this contractor and her passion for the environment certainly affected the practice, but also taught me much that I still use in my personal life. These changes also greatly affected the cleaners we contracted for the office. They now run a very successful eco-friendly cleaning service.

As this contractor moved on for family reasons, I began the whole process over again. The second time I felt wiser and more confident with the processes I was using to grow the practice. However, I did make some changes. I decided that, in the interest of my succession plan, I was looking this time for a younger counsellor who I could mentor and then pass the practice over to, setting her up for a successful future.

Pharsalus Amplexus
Embracing Professionalism

SECTION 4
ENDURING

CHAPTER 21
SYNERGY

When ducks fly, they form a V. This is to share the workload of flying. They cooperate, taking turns in leading, resting in the flanks when tired. If a duck cannot fly, due to injury, other ducks will break formation and stay with it until they can all fly again, never leaving one duck behind. When you think about it, it is really compassionate and caring for their fellow ducks. This is synergy. As a profession, counselling could learn from the ducks. If every counsellor spent time at the front of the V, being a leader and other counsellors all benefitted from the draught gaining ground without struggling, how amazing would the profession be! This is synergy.

Lawyers do synergy quite well. The stronger, more experienced lawyers take the lead. They use juniors to do their legwork, teaching them along the way. The juniors sit in court with the lawyers, learning their trade. Their leaders mentor them in the profession and they learn by participating in the practice of their profession. They are able to make mistakes and learn from them. At the same time, having someone to do the legwork for them enables the lawyers to do better work themselves. Like the ducks, it is a win-win situation. There is then a natural progression through the profession as, over time, lawyers develop into experts themselves. During the process, even the juniors are encouraged to lead at times.

The counselling profession could benefit from a system such as this. Many times, I have had phone calls and emails from students and new graduates asking for work experience. I hear the frustration in their request. At first, I would invite these graduates to sit in on any workshops I was holding, encouraging them to participate, as they felt comfortable. I felt this was not enough and most were looking for more than I was offering.

I, like many, thought I could not have students in a counselling session with me for confidentiality reasons. Then, one day, I decided that this was a belief that was limiting both the student seeking experience and me. How was I so sure that a student could not teach me a few things? They were learning the latest in their education; I could learn from them. I could also teach them from the experience and the knowledge I had gained over time. Together, using synergy, we could benefit my clients.

Sure, there would have to be some structure and boundaries to enable this to work, but I was confident it could work. I thought long and hard about how this would best work and wrote a procedure to use for students and graduates looking for experience. There was a lot to consider. Most students did not expect payment and were just grateful for the opportunity; however, some graduates requested payment for their services. I also felt that there should be a program to follow where we achieved gradual involvement with the clients and the student. The first session the student attended was not necessarily the first for the client and was purely an observation session for the student. I felt it necessary also to put some physical distance in this session so as not to distract the client. I was lucky in this to have a large office. The next couple of sessions were more inclusive with the student moving closer and offering information only when asked. After this, I fully integrated the student into the session. I made the student aware of certain restrictions and sensitivities that having two practitioners in a session may have on the client. I also was very clear that the client would always be my priority, and if I asked the student to leave, they would do so immediately.

The next time a student approached me for work experience, I invited her in for an interview. I had to be sure I could work well with her and that she agreed with the boundaries I would impose. She came with a set of rules of her own, set by the university and accompanied by a file of paperwork. We worked through both sets of rules and decided that we could work together. All I had to do was work my schedule of clients so that once a week I saw clients who would agree to have a student present in the room. This was easy to accomplish as I limited the number of clients for the day to four. I was determined to give a rounded education to this student, including note writing, practice administration and program writing.

The four clients who agreed to work in this program were all very supportive of the process, and why not? They were getting two professionals for the price of one. I designed a permission form for these clients and had the students sign a confidentiality contract that I gave to each of them.

For the six weeks that I had this student at the practice, I felt energised and looked forward to the days she attended the practice. We worked well with each other and fulfilled all the requirements of her university. We also covered much more than this, including ethical boundaries and practices and I felt I had mentored this student well. She interacted well with the clients and was genuinely interested in the running of the practice. She later approached me as a supervisor once she had graduated and I was happy to cooperate.

Most importantly, though, my clients benefitted from her presence in the sessions. One of the clients, who was suffering from a chronic illness, greatly appreciated some research I asked the student to do between sessions on meditation for pain relief. The student discussed this with the client during one of our sessions and referred the client to a meditation clinic for chronic illness. The client was very receptive and grateful.

Another of the clients, a child of seven years old, really connected with the student and, fortunately, her last session at the practice was the client's last session too. I think if he had come for more sessions, he would have missed the student.

Overall, this was a very successful experience for all involved and I was pleased to be the leading duck. This sort of synergy on an ongoing basis would greatly benefit the profession. Imagine having the same student every year of their study, having them become familiar with the practice and then joining the practice on graduation. After gaining experience this counsellor could then be the leader of the flight and mentor another student. Practices would evolve into multi-counsellor practices and exist longer than the working life of the original counsellor. The profession would be more cohesive and knowledge would be shared.

This may not be the desire of every counsellor, to work in synergy with others, and, in fact, I recognise the arguments against this. One that a counsellor discussed with me recently was the inevitability of spending time mentoring another counsellor who then opens a practice in competition. I understand this fear. In reality, though, this student was always going to practice. Some people make better employees than private practitioners though, and if a thorough process to choose students to mentor is in place then the right person can easily be found. I also feel that there is plenty of counselling work for everyone and competition is a motivator to improve our services and is healthy for the profession. If we mentor and this raises the standard of counselling, through both the sharing of knowledge and competition, then the profession is the real winner.

CHAPTER 22
SHARING

"I have written a really great worksheet for kids with anxiety," a graduate counsellor recently said to me at an Association meeting.

As I worked with children a lot, I was interested in a worksheet such as this, and was duly impressed that this counsellor had created a worksheet. I was interested, not because I wanted to 'steal' it but to discuss it and compare it to worksheets I had created for the same purpose, to gain mutual benefit via sharing. When I suggested we get together to share the logic of our worksheets, the response was, "Well, yours is probably better." Share does not mean compare. Share does not mean judge and definitely does not mean steal. A wealth of knowledge and strategic expertise is being lost through not sharing. I felt that by being interested in his worksheet I might encourage and support this counsellor, I might also learn from him.

The profession that does this really well is once again the law profession; in fact, it depends and thrives on sharing. Imagine what civil law would look like if no precedence existed, if there were no historical cases recorded and shared. I am positive not all people involved in these cases appreciate the sharing, but the wisdom and strategic thinking of the judges is valued by the profession—and also by society.

Our profession has some basic differences to the legal profession; confidentiality creates limitations to sharing. However, the sharing of knowledge gained in the field is very limited. There are papers and articles to read, seminars on the different modalities and workshops on how to utilise some strategies. Imagine what it would be like if we shared our successes and, yes, our non-successes. Imagine if, like the legal profession, we had a history of clients with a certain issue comparing how they progressed through counselling.

If a client presented at a practice with pet grief, for example. If we also presume the attending counsellor had little or no experience dealing with a client who had lost a pet and needed to upskill. The main avenue for this is presently to google. While this can be beneficial, as professionals, we need to be wary and to weed out the misinformation. How much more professional would it be if we had a database, like the civil law cases, where we could find a history of cases and their outcomes? I feel a responsibility to the profession to share my experiences. I have a great deal of experience in dealing with pet grief. This may enable someone to help a client, may prevent trial and error, and may educate counsellors to the possibility of options in their practices. Counsellors would have an instant research resource. Surely, it is in the best interest of our clients to share more in our profession.

If sharing in the counselling profession simply means talking in our small groups, or running regular tool shop type meetings, this needs to be encouraged a lot more than it is now. I do think we need to do more than this, though, to both grow as a profession and to gain public recognition as professionals united in knowledge.

Sharing is about more than professional expertise. The counselling profession overprotects intellectual property, but when we look at the business side of running a practice, we find a tendency towards secrecy. We guard our referral lists, our marketing successes and our supporters in our practices. A new practitioner stares at a blank canvas that is daunting. As a profession, we do little to assist or even encourage new practitioners, one can only assume for fear of competition. Imagine a counsellor or psychologist attempting to set up a practice and having a database available to them to help. A database that included accountants that specialise in counselling practices, IT specialists that understand our profession and lists of other professionals recommended by counsellors for referrals. Counsellors could view this list as a starting point and still do their due diligence in creating their own teams. This would be a great launch pad for a new practitioner. At a time when we need to make a large number of decisions, counsellors would find an asset like this invaluable. This is also a great way of supporting the people who support our profession. An accountant who specialises in our industry can simplify work for us by setting up a suitable accounting system and minimise our taxation. Finding such an accountant can be a long, frustrating process without recommendations. My accountant is a genius when it comes to taxation accounting; her help in decisions like the type of company I wanted to become, how I should employ counsellors and the best valuation to sell my practice saved me stress, time and money. I would happily recommend her to other counsellors so they too could benefit from her wisdom and knowledge.

This type of database needs the permission of the professionals involved and someone would have to monitor it and keep it up to date. A state-by-state, national and international database would be of enormous benefit. In this technological age, geography is no boundary for databases like this. It would benefit both new practitioners and existing ones who experience changes and growth. As a profession, we should encourage new and growing practices. These are the future of the profession.

CHAPTER 23
SUPPORT

Experience, no matter how extensive, does not preclude the need for support. It is obvious that new practitioners benefit from support. We can logically extend this need for support to growing practices. What is not so obvious is the need for support for the experienced, hopefully competent and confident practitioner. In our industry, no one is bulletproof. As counsellors become more experienced, maybe even become supervisors and deal with the more complex issues in counselling, there is a greater need for support. The simple fact that a counsellor is experienced does not mean that they become an island and isolate themselves from support. Sure, the type of support may change in character, but the need will still exist.

Our profession does not recognise experience. All members of the associations are just members. There are no fellowships or life members. Therefore, there is no peer support for these pillars of our profession. Other professions, like engineers, through their professional body can apply and have their association recognise them as Fellowes. This title allows other members to recognise the service and experience achieved by this professional. We need this sort of support from the Association as well.

The lack of support is true also for counsellors at a supervisory level, where peer support and supervision is up to the members and the associations give little or no guidance. Peer supervision for supervisors is an extremely logical and supportive process that enables sharing and learning at an elevated level. However, it is neither mandatory nor encouraged.

No matter what level of experience a counsellor has achieved, support from supervisors is available within the current counselling profession. To achieve the maximum impact of supervision, counsellors need to engage in the process; seek the support they require; play an active role in deciding how the supervisor can best support them. The minimum requirement of associations (10 hours/annum in the ACA) is often all that is undertaken. I find this distressing when I look at some of my supervisees who would benefit greatly from more interaction with experienced counsellors. I watch some of these same counsellors at Association meetings, intent on having their card signed off for their supervision and professional development at the cost of networking with the resources available at these meetings. There are usually a couple of supervisors, guest speakers, and an abundance of counsellors, psychologists and social workers in attendance. This is an underutilised resource for counsellors and there needs to be a shift in the mentality towards sharing, support and synergy.

I would like to touch here very briefly on the issue of compassion fatigue in so much as support is one of the remedies available for both prevention and treatment. Many counsellors are quite oblivious to the dangers of compassion fatigue. This is primarily because during their years of education there is no mention of compassion fatigue. I only realised this was true when I presented a talk to fourth year allied health students at one of our local universities. There was a group of allied health students including counsellors, paramedics, dentists, medical imagery and pharmacy, who were taking jobs in the rural districts. There was a group of about fifty students and when I enquired about how many students knew what compassion fatigue actually was; only three students raised their hands. Furthermore, when I asked for their definitions, they were all confused as to exactly what compassion fatigue was.

I was amazed that these students, in at risk professions, with the added complication of rural isolation, were uneducated in this risk to their work and their health. I have given the same presentation twice now to groups of counsellors and I found the ignorance of this threat was almost through the entire two groups.

In my role as a supervisor, with clients, and in my volunteer role at a native animal rescue not-for-profit, I have dealt with compassion fatigue quite regularly. The carer's curse, the combination of traumatic stress and burnout occurs in counselling. I often reflect on a quote from Rachel Renem—"*The expectation that we can be immersed in suffering and loss daily and not be touched by it is as unrealistic as expecting to be able to walk through water without getting wet.*" In our roles as counsellors, compassion fatigue is a real risk. The question at the end of each working day becomes "*How wet am I?*"

Support for compassion fatigue comes in three forms. Firstly, in education. As a profession, we need to be educated about compassion fatigue and its affect. Secondly, in our networks and practices, we need to be able to recognise changes in our colleagues and their behaviour that may indicate that they are 'getting wet'. The final form of support comes when we recognise compassion fatigue, to actually act and help our colleagues. This is particularly helpful if you share a workplace with other counsellors or meet regularly with them. I feel strongly that supervisors should have training in recognising the symptoms of compassion fatigue, largely because we do have regular, ongoing contact with our counsellors.

I have found over my time as a member of a professional association that I benefitted by being proactive and making a connection with the association. Many counsellors know little of their association, are unaware of the great information available from them and seem to enjoy a distance from their association. Only when we support our association do we feel the strength of their support for us. The local branch of the Association runs an interactive program where the more you put in, and network, the more you gain. Support is definitely a two-way street in this situation.

CHAPTER 24
SUCCESSION

The whole premise of this book has been to discuss the possibility of setting up, growing and operating a practice with the intention that it will endure. To enable this outcome, as we have seen, there needs to be some solid planning. Planning a business with the end in mind complicates the start-up process for sure, but will mean a smoother running practice once completed. Even with all the planning and forethought I put in before opening my practice, I could have done several things better. Spend the time and energy up front and you will limit the stress of running a practice.

This planning applies on both a personal and a business level. The need to be the best person, in the best headspace for the job, is important. The concept of counselling from a place of personal experience contaminates our promise to honour our client's individuality. The book has looked at becoming the best you for practicing. This is certainly more complex than just reading the book and doing the exercises. Believe in the process of our profession and work with a counsellor for your own benefit. It will benefit your practice.

Building a practice plan that includes the nine Ps – preliminaries, purpose, products, price, place, promotion, people, processes and profitability – gives your practice an extremely solid foundation. Including the flexibility that allows growth and change is important even at the planning stage. I recognise that for many counsellors this kind of thinking and organising is foreign, but I also believe, with the right structure to follow, it is also achievable for most people. Even if we struggle with some of the business concepts, we have the ability to surround ourselves with the right people in our team to help us.

The ethical side of counselling also needs consideration. Setting clear boundaries, both fixed and flexible, will prevent problems from arising as you practise. We all learn along the way, but learning inside these boundaries makes for better practitioners.

When it comes to the actual practising, I feel the most impact on the practice comes from networking, using supervision and professional development as stepping-stones rather than necessities, This means supporting one another and sharing. As a profession, sharing, supporting and working with synergy is the road forward. Through these skills, we will grow a stronger, cohesive and cooperative profession for the future.

These same characteristics build enduring practices. When we support new talent into the profession, share the knowledge of experience, treasure that knowledge, keep it safe for the future, and move as one towards the goal of professionalism, we will be accepted and appreciated as professionals. The new graduate will not encounter the same difficulties in setting up a practice. If we mentor students into the practice philosophy of sharing, support and synergy, it will empower them to build a team of best people around them. The completion of study will no longer mean being thrown into a void where they must search blindly for answers. The opportunity to buy into an existing successful practice, have someone hold your hand for a short while and explore the concepts with a safety net is very attractive and, importantly, constructive. Having experienced counsellors share their knowledge and strategies is invaluable in developing an ever-evolving profession.

I hear still, in the back of my mind, counsellors saying they do not have enough work to share; that it is difficult to get clients; that it is too competitive; that they do not have the knowhow to run a successful practice. Much discussion needs to happen for this type of change to occur. We need to build belief – at all levels, from students and new practitioners to existing practitioners and including our associations – that counselling as a profession that can achieve success and succession.

To actually sell your practice involves the making of many decisions. Many of these decisions were outside the scope of my knowledge and I relied heavily on my support team, particularly my accountant. If your succession plan includes the mentoring of a counsellor to take over the practice, plan this from the start.

I sold my practice. I continue to mentor in that practice, though less and less. I share my knowledge and strategies with those I supervise and with those included within my networks, even in semi-retirement. I believe counselling can advance, increasing in professionalism, overcome the doubts and lack of confidence both by counsellors and in counsellors and stand with and as an equal with other mental health professions.

Partem, favorem, synergy
Share, support, synergy

MY MISTAKES

Ok, time to confess. Along the way, I discovered a lot about myself. I made many mistakes over the years of practicing and learned many lessons. I thought it might help to share some of these. So, here goes:

1. In the early days of practice, I was very keen and motivated. I would have several projects on the go at the same time. This would lead me to become overwhelmed, and thus unproductive. I discovered that focus was important, as was the dealing with one job at a time. I began organising my time. Planning was once again the answer.
2. When I first opened the practice, my first clients came from a free talk I gave at the local high school. I was thrilled with the flow of clients this achieved. I gave several more free talks and gained clients each time. At some stage, I needed to value these talks. Yes, they were a source of clients but they were also a service to the clients.

I began charging for these talks and payment was never questioned. There was no difference between the free talks and the paid ones, except to my bank account.

3. Early on, I would be checking emails as they arrives. The ping of the inbox was exciting. As I got busier, that same ping became a distraction. I decided to dedicate two, half hour slots each day to emails. I turned off the ping and turned on the focus. I also scheduled my social media time as I found this to be a great time waster.

4. When the phone rings with a new client, it is very easy to confuse the two roles we perform in our practices. It took me a while to realise that when we answer the phones we are in receptionist role. I guess that part of me that wanted to help others would take over and I would find myself doing a phone consultation. One day I was on the phone to an inquiry about anxiety, and before I knew what was occurring, I had given the client several strategies. The client ended the call by saying that if these strategies did not work, then they would call for an appointment. I had completed a phone session free. I never heard back from that client.

5. I am often talking with my foot in my mouth. In my endeavour to listen effectively to my client, I often put a response together too quickly. One day I had a client whose husband had an issue with a dress she had bought. She had continually described the dress as elegant. As I summarised what I had heard from the client, I became tongue-tied and mistakenly called the dress an "elephant dress" instead of an "elegant dress". While the client was taken aback initially, we did eventually find the funny side to my faux pas.

6. I am a pleaser. While therapeutically speaking, I would not have a client leave at the end of a session in distress, I realised after a couple of years of practising that I was trying to have the clients leave pleased with their session. This was incongruent with the work the client sometimes had to do in a session. Eventually the penny dropped: my client does not have to like me; we only need rapport to achieve the desired outcomes. Recognising this allowed me to focus fully on the needs of the client.

7. I thought to postpone a session with a client was both unethical and unprofessional. I was to find that sometimes the opposite is true. One particular day, I attended the funeral of a friend. I left a good two hours after the funeral before my first appointment. I was unprepared for the impact of the funeral. I tried extremely hard to focus on the client in that first appointment, but I had definitely not shown up ready to work. I struggled through the session and when it was over, I knew I had not been the best me for that client. On reflection, I decided that postponing that session would have been preferable.

8. One of my biggest regrets in my practice was that I did not embrace social media as a tool for both advertising and networking. For someone with little knowledge of techy stuff, I allowed fear of the unknown to short change my practice. I often wonder at the impact social media might have had. I began embracing social media briefly before retiring and recognised that it could be beneficial to a practice.

9. When a client did not show for a session, I would get concerned. I felt that it was due to something

I had said or done. I would always give the client the benefit of the doubt. I would call and apologise for them not attending their session! Sometimes the client would reschedule their appointment and other times not. When they did not I would look at the previous session, searching for a reason for them. I learned to accept that sometimes clients just decided not to continue for reasons of their own. It had nothing to do with me.

10. In my initial consultation sign up form, I had a paragraph about cancellations that stated that cancellations within twenty-four-hours of the appointment or no-shows would attract the normal session fee. My time had value. Naturally, I made exceptions to this rule when events were unavoidable. I would however enforce this if clients just forgot an appointment or just decided not to attend. I would mail out an invoice and follow up with a phone call if payment was not received. I realised after a while that these phone calls were not only a waste of my time, but were bad public relations for the practice. Clients would not return for sessions with this approach. It seemed pointless

11. It has only been in retirement when I agreed to locum for the new owner of my business while she was on leave, that I realised a big mistake I had made. I had always worked really long hours before taking leave, and on my return. I had closed the practice when I was away and new clients would have to wait until I was back. This was definitely doing things the hard way. When I was locum, the counsellor could relax; I answered the phones and saw new clients. There was no stress

while on holidays. I recognise now how much I needed this stress-free relaxation.

12. When selling my practice, I was very aware that I wanted the new owner to accept and run the practice as I had done. I found myself questioning everything the new owner did differently. I finally decided that this should be a learning experience for the practice and I needed to let go! After so long, it was not mine to control.

THE BEST PRACTICE PROGRAM

"You must be the change you wish to see in the world"
Mahatma Gandhi

Best Practice, the book, is just the beginning! Join our group working with the concepts of Synergy, Sharing and Support. Become a member of our Best Practice Program, which is a collaborative counselling community and be a part of the change.

What the Best Practices Program delivers:

- An easy to follow plan for becoming the best you for your practice
- A step by step pro-forma practice building plan
- Weekly communication with your mentor
- Information sharing
- Support of your mentor and other members of the program

For information go to:
www.merrilynhughes.com/BestPracticeProgram

ACKNOWLEDGEMENTS

I am delighted to have an opportunity to acknowledge the people in my life, without whom BEST PRACTICES would still be an idea and an unfulfilled dream.

To my husband Trevor, thanks for backing me in yet another venture. Your support has enabled me to seek my destiny. To my four children, Bianca, Claire, Shane and Sophie, thank you for your encouragement. You and your partners have been a constant motivation. My gorgeous grandbabies, Ryley and Milla, are the reason I strive to achieve. I love you all.

I must thank my beta-readers, Angela, Bianca, Claire and Alison. Your contribution and encouragement have kept me motivated. I appreciate your work.

To my Fiverr editor Ken, your help, patience and professionalism have made this process in my first book an enjoyable experience. I appreciate your promptness and professionalism. Thank you.

To my publisher Kary Oberbrunner thanks for the ignition. Your knowledge, enthusiasm and caring have made this journey a joy. I could not have done this without you. To the Tribe – WOW! It has been my privilege and pleasure to get to know you all, to support you and to have you as support. This is a force to be reckoned with. I wish you all well for the future.

Finally, to all the counsellors who have inspired me to write this book. We have a profession to be proud of and one that has a future that we can influence every day we work. I would particularly like to thank those whom I supervise. Your challenges are my challenges and we will prevail!

MERRILYN'S PAGE

This is where I am supposed to write all about me. This book has the essence of my professional life as a counsellor and I feel shows many of my values as a person. My parents instilled in me an incredible work ethic. My mother's words "A job worth doing is worth doing well," have always kept me focused on being the best me I could be. One of my main roles in life has been as a mother and I am proud to say this same work ethic abounds in our next generation. I have four children who never had to be woken up and motivated to work, who have achieved at whatever they have tackled and of whom I am extremely proud.

Of my many roles in life, being an author feels like being home to me. I have thrived through this process and I am positive that this has been a personal growth period for me. I feel my retirement from my counselling practice has opened new doors for me, quite unexpectedly. My life's journey has prepared me for this book and hopefully others.

I am extremely proud to think that I may be giving back with this book. Counselling as a profession gave me so much and I hope I can repay the debt. The profession is still really in infant stages and the mother in me hopes I have nurtured it a little.

I hope you gain growth from BEST PRACTICE.

Connect to me: merrilynhughes.com
Contact me: merrilyn@merrilynhughes.com